S.O.S. FOR WORDPERFECT™

by Katherine Murray

IDG BOOKS

IDG Books Worldwide, Inc.
An International Data Group Company

San Mateo, California ✦ Indianapolis, Indiana ✦ Boston, Massachusetts

S.O.S. For WordPerfect

Published by
IDG Books Worldwide, Inc.
An International Data Group Company
155 Bovet Road, Suite 310
San Mateo, CA 94402

Library of Congress Catalog Card No.: 93-080871

ISBN: 1-56884-053-5

Printed in the United States of America

10 9 8 7 6 5 4 3 2 1

Distributed in the United States by IDG Books Worldwide, Inc.

Distributed in Canada by Macmillan of Canada, a Division of Canada Publishing Corporation; by Computer and Technical Books in Miami, Florida, for South America and the Caribbean; by Longman Singapore in Singapore, Malaysia, Thailand, and Korea; by Toppan Co. Ltd. in Japan, by Asia Computerworld in Hong Kong; by Woodslane Pty. Ltd. in Australia and New Zealand; and by Transworld Publishers Ltd. in the U.K. and Europe.

For information on where to purchase IDG Books outside the U.S., contact Christina Turner at 415-312-0633. For information on translations, contact Marc Jeffrey Mikulich, Foreign Rights Manager, at IDG Books Worldwide; FAX NUMBER 415-358-1260.

For sales inquiries and special prices for bulk quantities, write to the address above or call IDG Books Worldwide at 415-312-0650.

Dedication

To Doug, who makes everything possible

Acknowledgments

Egad — another book. This one, like the others, is a mesh of the talents of some incredibly gifted people, including

David Solomon, Publisher, for his initial vision and for his ability to balance the possible with the impossible — and then achieve both.

Laurie Smith, Project Editor, for seeing in this series possibilities that no one else saw, and for single-sightedly making sure they evolved into the best reality she could ask for them, given an extremely limited amount of time and under several oppressive deadlines.

Christopher Rozzi, Illustrator, for taking his characters — and us — through yet another incredibly imaginative journey,

John Kaufeld, Consulting Writer, for his terrific job on writing the chapters on fonts and printing (and in such a timely manner) and for his overall development comments that helped us keep the focus of the book,

Cynthia Mikeworth, Technical Editor, for checking the technical accuracy of the manuscript and helping us ensure that we came up with as many antidotes as possible,

Claudette Moore, of Moore Literary Agency, for being the counterweight of reason to my temporary insanities,

Beth Jenkins and Bill Hartman, for their unrelenting pursuit of the ultimate design, and Cindy Phipps, Valery Bourke, Gina Scott, and the rest of the Production department, for all of their hard work and patience,

Julie King, Tim Gallan, Shawn MacLaren, Sharon Hilgenberg, and Sandy Grieshop for their unfailing and unflagging attention to detail.

My family — Doug, Kelly, Christopher, and Cameron — for Taco Bell on late work nights and good report cards and quiet sleepovers and Lego mansions and quick 2:00 a.m. feedings.

Katherine Murray

(The publisher would like to give special thanks to Patrick J. McGovern, without whom this book would not have been possible.)

About IDG Books Worldwide

Welcome to the world of IDG Books Worldwide.

IDG Books Worldwide, Inc., is a division of International Data Group, the world's largest publisher of computer-related information and the leading global provider of information services on information technology. IDG publishes over 194 computer publications in 62 countries. Forty million people read one or more IDG publications each month.

If you use personal computers, IDG Books is committed to publishing quality books that meet your needs. We rely on our extensive network of publications, including such leading periodicals as *Macworld*, *InfoWorld*, *PC World*, *Computerworld*, *Publish*, *Network World*, and *SunWorld*, to help us make informed and timely decisions in creating useful computer books that meet your needs.

Every IDG book strives to bring extra value and skill-building instruction to the reader. Our books are written by experts, with the backing of IDG periodicals, and with careful thought devoted to issues such as audience, interior design, use of icons, and illustrations. Our editorial staff is a careful mix of high-tech journalists and experienced book people. Our close contact with the makers of computer products helps ensure accuracy and thorough coverage. Our heavy use of personal computers at every step in production means we can deliver books in the most timely manner.

We are delivering books of high quality at competitive prices on topics customers want. At IDG, we believe in quality, and we have been delivering quality for over 25 years. You'll find no better book on a subject than an IDG book.

John Kilcullen
President and C.E.O.
IDG Books Worldwide, Inc.

IDG Books Worldwide, Inc. is a division of International Data Group. The officers are Patrick J. McGovern, Founder and Board Chairman; Walter Boyd, President. International Data Group's publications include: ARGENTINA's Computerworld Argentina, InfoWorld Argentina; ASIA's Computerworld Hong Kong, PC World Hong Kong, Computerworld Southeast Asia, PC World Singapore, Computerworld Malaysia, PC World Malaysia; AUSTRALIA's Computerworld Australia, Australian PC World, Australian Macworld, Network World, Reseller, IDG Sources; AUSTRIA's Computerwelt Oesterreich, PC Test; BRAZIL's Computerworld, Mundo IBM, Mundo Unix, PC World, Publish; BULGARIA's Computerworld Bulgaria, Ediworld, PC & Mac World Bulgaria; CANADA's Direct Access, Graduate Computerworld, InfoCanada, Network World Canada; CHILE's Computerworld, Informatica; COLOMBIA's Computerworld Colombia; CZECH REPUBLIC's Computerworld, Elektronika, PC World; DENMARK's CAD/CAM WORLD, Communications World, Computerworld Danmark, LOTUS World, Macintosh Produktkatalog, Macworld Danmark, PC World Danmark, PC World Produktguide, Windows World; EQUADOR's PC World; EGYPT's Computerworld (CW) Middle East, PC World Middle East; FINLAND's MikroPC, Tietoviikko, Tietoverkko; FRANCE's Distributique, GOLDEN MAC, InfoPC, Languages & Systems, Le Guide du Monde Informatique, Le Monde Informatique, Telecoms & Reseaux; GERMANY's Computerwoche, Computerwoche Focus, Computerwoche Extra, Computerwoche Karriere, Information Management, Macwelt, Netzwelt, PC Welt, PC Woche, Publish, Unit; HUNGARY's Alaplap, Computerworld SZT, PC World, ; INDIA's Computers & Communications; ISRAEL's Computerworld Israel, PC World Israel; ITALY's Computerworld Italia, Lotus Magazine, Macworld Italia, Networking Italia, PC World Italia; JAPAN's Computerworld Japan, Macworld Japan, SunWorld Japan, Windows World; KENYA's East African Computer News; KOREA's Computerworld Korea, Macworld Korea, PC World Korea; MEXICO's Compu Edicion, Compu Manufactura, Computacion/Punto de Venta, Computerworld Mexico, MacWorld, Mundo Unix, PC World, Windows; THE NETHERLAND'S Computer! Totaal, LAN Magazine, MacWorld; NEW ZEALAND's Computer Listings, Computerworld New Zealand, New Zealand PC World; NIGERIA's PC World Africa; NORWAY's Computerworld Norge, C/World, Lotusworld Norge, Macworld Norge, Networld, PC World Ekspress, PC World Norge, PC World's Product Guide, Publish World, Student Data, Unix World, Windowsworld, IDG Direct Response; PANAMA's PC World; PERU's Computerworld Peru, PC World; PEOPLES REPUBLIC OF CHINA's China Computerworld, PC World China, Electronics International, China Network World; IDG HIGH TECH BEIJING's New Product World; IDG SHENZHEN's Computer News Digest; PHILLIPPINES' Computerworld, PC World; POLAND's Computerworld Poland, PC World/Komputer; PORTUGAL's Cerebro/PC World, Correio Informatico/Computerworld, MacIn; ROMANIA's PC World; RUSSIA's Computerworld-Moscow, Mir-PC, Sety; SLOVENIA's Monitor Magazine; SOUTH AFRICA's Computing S.A.; SPAIN's Amiga World, Computerworld Espana, Communicaciones World, Macworld Espana, NeXTWORLD, PC World Espana, Publish, Sunworld; SWEDEN's Attack, ComputerSweden, Corporate Computing, Lokala Natverk/LAN, Lotus World, MAC&PC, Macworld, Mikrodatorn, PC World, Publishing & Design (CAP), Datalngenjoren, Maxi Data, Windows World; SWITZERLAND's Computerworld Schweiz, Macworld Schweiz, PC & Workstation; TAIWAN's Computerworld Taiwan, Global Computer Express, PC World Taiwan; THAILAND's Thai Computerworld; TURKEY's Computerworld Monitor, Macworld Turkiye, PC World Turkiye; UNITED KINGDOM's Lotus Magazine, Macworld, Sunworld; UNITED STATES' AmigaWorld, Cable in the Classroom, CD Review, CIO, Computerworld, Desktop Video World, DOS Resource Guide, Electronic News, Federal Computer Week, Federal Integrator, GamePro, IDG Books, InfoWorld, InfoWorld Direct, Laser Event, Macworld, Multimedia World, Network World, NeXTWORLD, PC Games, PC Letter, PC World Publish, Sumeria, SunWorld, SWATPro, Video Event; VENEZUELA's Computerworld Venezuela, MicroComputerworld Venezuela; VIETNAM's PC World Vietnam

About the author

Long on the receiving end of computer problems, Katherine Murray has been a computer user since the early '80s, when, at home with an infant daughter and an 8088, she began a writing career that would eventually take her through 37 computer books, across platforms (PC and Mac), and into a world of computer trouble. She enjoys writing the S.O.S. series because it gives her a chance to commiserate with other computer users who, like her, often "Panic first and think later."

About the consulting writer

John Kaufeld is a computer consultant, husband, and father to two very energetic toddlers (who recently developed a new game called "Sort Daddy's Manuscript"). He is a card-carrying witch doctor with computer experience dating back to when he thought Tandy Model Is with 4K of memory were a big deal. In both hours of his free time, he enjoys playing with his children, watching his wife sew, and playing railroad games with other equally flawed friends.

About the illustrator

Christopher Rozzi has illustrated several computer books in his free time, when he's not wearing his other hat as an indispensable exhibit artist at the Children's Museum in Indianapolis. He somehow managed to find the time to get married recently, which was amazing because we have kept him busy illustrating every hour of the day and night. Chris is an avid comic book collector, and he enjoys scuba diving, hiking, relaxing with his wife, Susan, and deciphering the various personalities of Lagniappe, their cat.

Credits

Publisher
David Solomon

Managing Editor
Mary Bednarek

Acquisitions Editor
Janna Custer

Production Manager
Beth Jenkins

Senior Editors
Sandy Blackthorn
Diane Graves Steele

Production Coordinator
Cindy L. Phipps

Acquisitions Assistant
Megg Bonar

Editorial Assistants
Patricia R. Reynolds
Darlene Cunningham

Project Editor
Laurie Ann Smith

Illustrator
Christopher Rozzi

Story Line
Christopher Rozzi
Laurie Ann Smith

Consulting Writer
John Kaufeld

Editors
Tim Gallan
Julie King
Shawn MacLaren

Technical Reviewer
Cynthia Mikeworth

Production Staff
Valery Bourke
Gina Scott

Proofreader
Sandy Grieshop

Indexer
Sharon Hilgenberg

Book Design
Beth Jenkins
William Hartman
Accent Technical
    Communications

Table of Contents

Prologue

Just when you thought it was safe to go back in the water . . . here you are marooned again. Actually, this time you can't blame storms or pirates; it was that blasted engine trouble. You have to remember next time that no matter how desperate you are, don't let someone convince you to go up in one of those small planes again. From now on, only DC-10s or 747s, and only first class. . . . (That is, of course, if you ever get out of here.)

Deep in the sea of technology lurk countless horrors you don't want to know about. Things like tabs and margins, formats and fonts, macros and merge prints.

Shhhh. Let's float by without waking them.

Once upon a time, communication involved a couple of grunts and maybe a scratch or two. Then communication went through an upgrade and settled in to a millennium of stick-in-sand writing. Then we moved up to stone tablets, cave walls — that sort of thing.

Today, we're expected to come up with eye-popping documents, spectacular designs, multicolumn formats, four-color graphics, and even real voice-recorded notes. And while we're doing it, we have to dodge those things with teeth — those styles and searches and setup problems.

That's an awful lot to expect from a person who, at this moment, can't even find a dry stick.

Welcome to S.O.S. For WordPerfect

Want to figure out your WordPerfect problem and get back on the road to happy — or at least not-miserable — computing? Look through this book a little bit. *S.O.S. For WordPerfect* includes quick, easy-to-get-to answers for those problems that no one wants to help you with (or you're too embarrassed to ask about).

This is it, folks.
Grab your parachute,
we're going down . . . .

S.O.S. For WordPerfect helps pull you in to shore, where you can investigate possible solutions or just get beyond the danger point — fast. And even though you'll find information on the biggest trouble spots — startup, formatting, mail merge, and so on — you won't find yourself drowning in esoteric references that don't apply to your particular predicament.

Navigating through the Book

This isn't a book that you'll read cover to cover. Who has time? When you're sinking, your only thought is "I'm sinking! How can I stop sinking?"

S.O.S. For WordPerfect is organized so that you can find your problem easily and get right to the answer. You can look up your problem in the table of contents or the index and go right to that point in the book. For example, if you are trying to change your tab settings and they are giving you fits, turn to Chapter 5, "Formatting Fiascoes," to find possible solutions.

If you *do* decide to read this book from start to finish (got some time on your hands, eh?), you'll be able to follow the story line that accompanies the illustrations. You'll also notice the cool sidebars:

Techie Terms	Definitions of the most appalling computerese (words and phrases)
Witch Doctors	Suggestions on how to deal with technical support masters
Satchels	Recipes for making stuff to put in your satchel so that you'll be better prepared for the future
Stepping Stones	Summarized steps for possible solutions
Smoke Signals	Error messages discussed nearby in the chapter
Words of Wisdom	Bits of witch doctor advice and extra tools that you can use to enhance WordPerfect
Road signs	Warnings and directions to help you on your way
Scroll	Basic (but secret) troubleshooting tenets that all the best witch doctors know

In the story line, you'll see the unfolding, heart-rending journey of one lost soul as he faces great adversity, struggling to survive in a land of confusion.

When You First Encounter WordPerfect

Part of the way you feel about WordPerfect depends on whether the decision to use it was one you made or one that was forced on you. If everyone in the office is switching over and you have no choice but to be dragged along, kicking and screaming, chances are that you won't be expecting a very pleasant experience. If you made the choice to shell out the few hundred bucks and get WordPerfect for your business or home office, you've got to justify your purchase, so you're hoping that it will be all you want it to be and more.

And boy, is it *more*. More options than you'll know what to do with. More ways to look at a single document than you can shake a stick at. More formatting choices than the average person should have to deal with in an entire lifetime.

Feel your pulse quicken? That's WordPerfect panic. That throbbing in your temples? Mail merge migraines.

People deal with stress in different ways: For the totally repressed, some heavy-duty gum chewing works wonders. For the uninhibited, high sustained shrieks seem to work very well. Throwing your WordPerfect manuals out the window (if you can lift that much weight) or even swearing and making rude gestures at your monitor is within the realm of acceptability.

But when you feel the need to *do something* — like stuff the computer down the mail chute — get up and walk away. Wander around a little bit and listen in on the latest office gossip. Then, when you're feeling a little more yourself, get out your copy of *S.O.S. For WordPerfect* to help you find your answer.

Part 1

What Happened? Where Am I?

After matching up with the witch doctor (and floating around for who knows how long), you finally spot land. Looks like another island. Better head for shore. Cold, bedraggled, and exhausted, you decide to swim for it nonetheless. But look at the witch doctor. He always seems to be better off. He looks so darned smug and comfortable. He says he'll take his time and just float that way. He'll catch up to you later. Yeah, sure — as long as there aren't any more hurricanes. . . .

Chapter 1

Off to a Bad Start

Paths through Peril

When taking those first few steps on unfamiliar ground, everything is frightening — from the smallest stinging insect to the largest land mammal. So it is with WordPerfect's installation and startup. It looks bad before you do it, but seems not so awful afterward.

You've always heard that skydiving is such an exhilarating experience.

But somehow, bailing out of a crashing plane just isn't the kind of excitement you had in mind.

Full-Up Hard Disk?

Poison: No room to install

Somebody walked in this morning, handed you the WordPerfect package, and said, "Dave wants you to use this to do the newsletter this week."

You open the package, take out the disks, and put the Install 1 disk in the drive. Everything seems to be going smoothly until WordPerfect pulls up short and says

```
The specified drive does not have enough room to install
all WordPerfect files.
```

What do you do?

Antidote: First, look carefully at the information WordPerfect is showing you. In fact, write it down. For a complete installation — with all WordPerfect's bells and whistles — you need a whopping 16MB of hard disk space. For a bones-only version, you need 7MB.

If you don't have 7MB free, consider trying the following things:

- Install WordPerfect on a different drive if you've got another hard disk or your disk is partitioned.

- Exit installation; remove any unnecessary programs and data; and return to WordPerfect to do (at least) the minimal installation.

- Clear away disk clutter with CHKDSK /F and DEFRAG (see the Words of Wisdom sidebar in this section for more information).

- Use a disk compression utility, like DoubleSpace (DOS 6.X) or Stacker, to squeeze the data you've got into a smaller space.

- Add another hard disk (unlikely, but worth a shot).

Whatever you do, don't elect to continue with the installation even though you don't have the room. You'll waste 15 or 20 minutes and then get an error message telling you that your disk is full. Not a fun way to spend a coffee break.

Custom Install Lite

Poison: Not knowing what to install

You don't have enough storage space for the whole 16MB WordPerfect program, so you've got to pick and choose the features you want. Trouble is, you've never used this program before. How are you supposed to know what you need and what you don't?

Antidote: When you choose Custom install, WordPerfect's install utility will first ask you to confirm the various directories that it will create during the installation process. Go ahead and complete that step, even if you don't think you'll install some of the features for which you're okaying directories.

After you select Exit, WordPerfect displays the Custom Installation screen. There's a checklist on the left showing all WordPerfect features loaded in a standard install. On the right side of the feature, the amount of the disk storage space used by the item is shown. On the right side of the screen, a message box tells you which features are integral to the operation of the program and which features are extras. You can decide what to keep and what to leave off by reading these messages. (A little common sense goes a

long way, too — don't install Fax Files if you don't have a fax or Sound Drivers if you don't have a sound board.)

Where's the Disk?

Poison: Repeated disk prompting

You started your Standard installation and kicked back to watch the prompts (what fun). Pretty soon your computer beeps an alarm and asks you to

```
Insert into drive B the master diskette labeled Install 2
```

You pop Install 2 into the drive and press Enter. Another beep, and

```
Insert into drive B the master diskette labeled Install 2
```

Wait a minute. Something's wrong here.

Antidote: If you're lucky, WordPerfect just didn't see your Enter keypress the first time, and trying again should alleviate the problem. If this isn't your lucky day, check the following things:

Install Pitfalls
When you choose Custom install, WordPerfect will let you do away with any group of files that you want, so be careful. If you accidentally uncheck files that you really need, WordPerfect may not run at all.

- *Do you have the right disk?* If someone else has installed the program before, the disks may be out of order. Make sure that the label name matches the requested name on-screen.

🦅 *Are the right files on the disk?* If you're using the originals from WordPerfect Corporation, you know you've got the right files. But if you made backup copies of the original disks before you started installation (like everybody tells you to do), it's possible that you affixed the wrong label to the disk or copied the wrong files to the right disk. To find out, type DIR B: (if the files are on the disk in drive B) and press Enter.

Words of Wisdom:

CHKDSK

Use the DOS CHKDSK command to clean extraneous bits of data off your hard disk. At the DOS prompt, type

```
CHKDSK /F
```

and press Enter. When DOS asks whether you want to convert the lost clusters to chains (don't ask what chains are), Just Say No. DOS will wipe away the data like it was never there.

DEFRAG

Okay, so CHKDSK wipes away the little data spills, but what can you do to tighten up the data so that you don't have pockets of blank space on your hard disk? (You *want* the blank space, but you want it in one continuous block.) Answer: Use DOS 6.X's **DEFRAG** command. At the DOS prompt, type DEFRAG, press Enter, and follow the colorful on-screen prompts to optimize your hard disk space.

🖙 *Is the disk damaged?* Oh, you can look for the tell-tale signs — a mean-looking fold down the middle, coffee stains, fingerprints — but most physical disk injuries aren't obvious ones. Try getting a file list by using the DIR command (DIR B: or DIR A:). If you get an `Error reading drive B` message, something's up with the disk. Before you throw in the towel (or the disk), see if your witch doctor has any tricks up his sleeve.

Mouseless Install

Poison: Missing mouse during installation

You've decided to roll up your shirtsleeves and do a custom install. You follow the prompts and things seem pretty normal. Then you get to the Custom Installation screen with its list of features and check boxes. You reach for the mouse to uncheck a box and . . . hey, wait . . . this mouse is dead.

Antidote: Even though WordPerfect lets you have your mouse friend for opening menus, choosing commands, and various and sundry other tasks, the installation utility isn't nearly so accommodating. No mouse, no how. To check and uncheck check boxes, highlight the item and press Enter.

Upgrade or Install?

Poison: Not sure how to go from from 5.1 to 6.0

You had a pet program: WordPerfect 5.1. Yes, you hate to admit it, but the program kind of grew on you. Now someone comes along and gives you WordPerfect 6.0. You're not sure what to do with it. Is this a kind of mystical add-on thing — you use the Install program and 5.1 just changes into 6.0 — or do you need to totally install WordPerfect 6.0?

Antidote: If you've ever upgraded to another version of a program (like from DOS 5 to DOS 6.X or from Windows 3.0 to Windows 3.1), you know that the installation utility just updates the old program. You don't have to sit through the long, boring, installation process.

WordPerfect 6.0 installation is more than an upgrade. In fact, WordPerfect 6.0 is so different from 5.1 that you may want to consider keeping both around for a while (if your hard disk can afford it). If you're used to using 5.1, some of the changes in 6.0 may throw you for a loop (a *good* loop).

Where's WordPerfect?

Poison: WordPerfect doesn't start

You finished installation. The clock's ticking. Fourteen minutes until the manager's meeting. Can you start the program, type a quick memo, have your assistant make copies, and get to the meeting in time? You type WP and press Enter and . . .

```
Bad command or file name
```

Looks like you won't be at that meeting in time.

Antidote: There could be several reasons why you see such a shutdown message on your first real encounter with WordPerfect:

- *Is the program installed?*

- *Was the program installed correctly?* (That is, did you — or whomever installed the program — use the install utility on the Install

1 disk to create the necessary directories and put the files on the hard disk? Just copying the files over won't work.)

▶ *During installation, when WordPerfect asked to modify your AUTOEXEC.BAT file, did you answer Yes?* This procedure adds a line to the PATH statement in your AUTOEXEC.BAT file that makes it possible for you to start WordPerfect from any directory on your hard drive.

▶ *If you answered No, are you in the WP60 directory?* If you didn't let WordPerfect modify your AUTOEXEC.BAT file, you need to change to the WP60 directory (type CD WP60 and press Enter) before you type WP to start WordPerfect.

Words of Wisdom: AUTOEXEC.BAT and CONFIG.SYS

Your PC uses two important files — AUTOEXEC.BAT and CONFIG.SYS — to set things up each time you start your computer. These two files are stored in the root directory of your hard disk (which is probably C:\) and should never be deleted.

CONFIG.SYS contains commands that take care of your computer's hardware (memory, mouse, keyboard, printer); AUTOEXEC.BAT contains the PATH statement for your programs, runs any automatic programs (like TSRs or memory managers), and takes care of the look of the DOS prompt.

If you check all these things and you still see Bad command or file name, consult your witch doctor. There's something fishy going on.

File Handle Trouble

Poison: File handle errors

The program is installed. You changed to the WP directory by typing CD WP60 and pressing Enter. You're ready to rock. You type WP, press Enter, and, instead of the opening screen, you see an error message about "file handles."

Antidote: A line in your CONFIG.SYS file that controls the number of file handles set up for your system. Although WordPerfect needs a minimum of 25 in order to run, WordPerfect Corporation recommends that you set the FILES= line in your CONFIG.SYS file to 30.

Techie Term

RAM is an acronym for random-access memory — sometimes called just *memory* — which is where your programs and data are temporarily located while you're working with them. RAM is kind of like a fast short-term memory area.

How do you edit CONFIG.SYS? Before you do anything, make a backup copy of the file in case you need to return to the unaltered version later. Then, if you've got DOS 5.0 or later, type EDIT CONFIG.SYS at the DOS prompt (root directory) and press Enter. The file appears on the screen and you can make the necessary changes.

If you're using a version of DOS pre-5.0, you've got to use a strange editor called EDLIN — see *DOS For Dummies*, by Dan Gookin, for details.

After you make the change, save the file and reboot your computer. There. That fixes the file handle problem.

How to Make a Boot Disk

When you're first starting out, it's hard to know what tools you need to help you out of tight spots. One trick in the witch doctor's bag is the boot disk.

If you are using a computer with a hard drive, you're accustomed to having everything start just the way it's supposed to. But someday you may find that your computer forgets the routine.

That's when the boot disk comes in handy.

The boot disk is a disk that has — already on it — the commands that your computer needs in order to start. You can create your own boot disk (while you're at it, make two — they're small) by inserting a blank diskette in drive A or B and typing the following command at the DOS prompt:

```
FORMAT A: /S
```

(If the disk is in drive B, use FORMAT B: /S instead.) DOS begins formatting your disk, and after the format is complete, it copies over the necessary startup commands. Now if your computer ever hangs itself during startup, you can slide that boot disk into place and reboot the system. And won't that witch doctor be impressed?

What Is a Witch Doctor?

When you finally do find some-one to help you with a computer problem, it's always kind of mysterious how he (or she) provides you with the solution.

These witch doctor types can offer some pretty strange rituals to go through to fix your problem; everything from ceremonial sacrifices to magic potions. You can't live without them though. I mean, what else are you gonna do when your computer gets possessed?

So go ahead and eat that crunchy bug if they tell you to (even if it tastes bad) because you may have no other choice. Before you do though, make sure that you've found a true witch doctor (there are lots of quacks you know). To learn how to find a good one, see Chapter 2.

For additional advice about how to facilitate your interactions with witch doctors (and hopefully increase the chances of solving your problem), look for these witch doctor sidebars throughout the book.

What? Not Enough Memory to Start?

Poison: No RAM to run

You type the necessary command at the prompt and eagerly await the WordPerfect opening screen. After a moment, you see a message, saying that your computer is too low on memory for the program to run.

Antidote: WordPerfect 6.0 makes no bones about memory requirements: you need at least 480K of conventional memory to start the program. If you plan to use the whole shebang — complete with Graphics and Page modes — try to free up 550K to avoid memory errors and painfully slow operation.

While trying to release captive RAM, consider these questions:

How much RAM do you have? You can find out by typing MEM at the DOS prompt and looking at the "largest executable program size" line. (This line tells you how much RAM you've got available for WordPerfect.)

Do you have any TSRs loaded? If you're not sure, reboot your computer and watch for on-screen messages. A TSR displays a message when it loads. If you suspect that you've got a TSR loading automatically, ask your witch doctor to come take a look at your AUTOEXEC.BAT file.

Did you use a memory manager to optimize memory? MEMMAKER is one example of a memory manager — a utility that helps you use your computer's memory in the most efficient way possible. To run MEMMAKER (DOS 6.X only), you type MEMMAKER at the DOS prompt and press Enter.

Have you tried using a startup switch? WordPerfect lets you use a number of different startup switches to control how the program is placed in memory. This feature can free up RAM that you need for program operation. For example, WP /R loads a portion of the WordPerfect program into either expanded or extended memory, whichever you have available.

If you've tried everything you can think of and you're still getting memory errors, consult the witch doctor. There may be something he can do that is beyond the capability of mere mortals.

The Ol' Switcheroo

Poison: Which switch?

You've got both expanded memory and extended memory on your system. But you're not sure which switch to use with WP at startup.

Antidote: The three switches that most directly affect the way WordPerfect loads into memory are

- /R, which loads program information into either expanded or extended, whatever your computer has available

- /RE, which loads information into expanded memory

- /RX, which loads information into extended memory

Words of Wisdom: MEMMAKER

If you have DOS 6 and a 386 or 486 machine, use MEMMAKER to make the most of your available memory. At the DOS prompt, type MEMMAKER and press Enter. Then follow the jolly on-screen prompt. Just remember to keep your cool — MEMMAKER takes care of all the rough stuff for you. When it's finished, MEMMAKER tells you how much memory it has saved you. Now WordPerfect should have a little more space.

WordPerfect has a whole slew of startup switches you can use. To list them all, type WP /H and press Enter.

Not Expanded Enough

Poison: Not enough expanded memory

You try to start WordPerfect with the /RE switch and, as WordPerfect starts, it tells you that there is not enough expanded memory to use /R (which includes both /RE and /RX).

Antidote: WordPerfect will go ahead and start anyway — there's nothing you need to do any differently. The block of expanded memory you were hoping to use to store some of your WordPerfect program information is just not big enough to hold anything significant. WordPerfect is saying "Thanks, but no thanks."

Techie Term

A *startup switch* is an additional parameter (command part such as /H) that you enter when you type WP to start WordPerfect. You can use a startup switch to control screen display, prompts, memory, macros, and other Word-Perfect features.

It's also possible that you *do* have enough expanded memory but your Expanded Memory Manager has not been installed or is malfunctioning. If you suspect that a problem with the Extended Memory Manager is causing the trouble, call your witch doctor for further enlightenment.

For the future, though, if you're just short on expanded memory, you may want to talk to your witch doctor about ways to optimize memory so that you will be able to use WordPerfect with the /R switch. Memory optimization can free up quite a bit of conventional memory, which can dramatically increase WordPerfect's overall speed.

How to Make a System Info Report

One good troubleshooting tool is a WordPerfect report that tells you about the various features of your system. What kind of microprocessor does your machine have? You don't know? What about the display type, the amount of RAM and expanded memory, the version of DOS you're running, and your disk drive types?

Still drawing a blank? A utility included with WordPerfect can clue you in. WPINFO.EXE is copied to your WP60 (or WP51) directory during installation. To use the utility, exit to DOS, change to your WordPerfect directory, and type

```
WPINFO
```

Then press Enter. The System Information screen appears, listing all the important characteristics of your system. To get a quick printout, make sure that your printer is on-line and ready and press Print Screen.

After you're finished readying the System Information screen, press a key and your AUTOEXEC.BAT file is displayed. Press another key, and you see your CONFIG.SYS file. You can't edit these files in WPINFO, but you can view them and get a quick print.

Keep a copy of the WPINFO report nearby in case you (or the witch doctor) ever need it to answer any questions about your system. Remember to print an updated copy of WPINFO anytime you add memory, reconfigure drives, upgrade DOS, change a monitor, or make other significant system changes.

Network Memory Fight

Poison: Memory conflict on a network

You just tried to start WordPerfect for the first time on the new network. Everything was supposed to work fine. But as you eagerly await the opening screen, you see

```
Network device fault on drive
```

Antidote: In some cases, WordPerfect suffers from expanded memory jitters when running on a network. Try these remedies to get around the problem:

- Start WordPerfect with the WP /32 startup switch. (The /32 startup switch uses a different memory specification at startup.) If that doesn't work,

- Try starting WordPerfect with the WP /NE command. (The /NE switch disables expanded memory use. If WordPerfect starts fine, you know the problem is with the memory manager and not with the network.) If that doesn't work,

- Try starting WordPerfect as a stand-alone system (if you've got the necessary program files on your system and they aren't kept as shared resources) by using the WP /SA switch. If WordPerfect runs fine as a

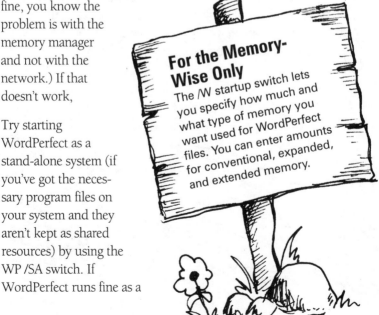

For the Memory-Wise Only
The /W startup switch lets you specify how much and what type of memory you want used for WordPerfect files. You can enter amounts for conventional, expanded, and extended memory.

stand-alone, you know that the problem has something to do with the network installation.

For more information on memory issues, see *InfoWorld WordPerfect 6 SECRETS*, by Roger C. Parker and David A. Holzgang (IDG, 1993).

Pushed-Too-Far WordPerfect

Poison: Not-enough-memory

WordPerfect started fine and you began creating your first document. You tried to view the document in Page mode and were jerked back to reality with the following message:

```
Not enough memory for graphics
```

And that just started the ball rolling. Seems like every time you turn around, you're running smack into Not-enough-memory errors.

Antidote: Yes, it can drive you crazy. Working with a feature-laden program when you're running short on RAM is a frustrating thing. Here are a few things that you can do when you just have to run WordPerfect on a computer with a limited amount of RAM:

If you started WordPerfect using the Shell, save your document, exit the program, and reboot. Then start WordPerfect again from the DOS prompt — without the Shell — by typing WP and pressing Enter.

Keep an eye on your available RAM by starting WordPerfect with the /WS startup switch.

Use Text mode (you won't be able to get into Graphics mode and Page mode anyway).

Put away the Ribbon, Button Bar, Scroll bars, and Outline bar.

Use few — or no — graphics boxes.

If you've got Hyphenation turned on, turn it off.

Select default graphics drivers instead of specialized or custom drivers.

At best, these memory-saving techniques are short-term fixes because they don't allow you to use the best features of WordPerfect (which you, or someone in your office, have already paid for). You have a significant argument for requesting more memory for your machine. Now, where is that system requisition?

Note: When your pulse returns to normal, check out *WordPerfect For Dummies*, by Dan Gookin. This book includes some almost-fun tips that you can try at startup. (Well, I said *almost*.)

Reading Smoke Signals

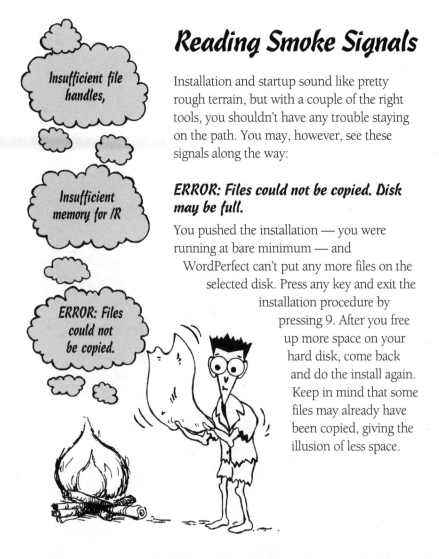

Insufficient file handles,

Insufficient memory for /R

ERROR: Files could not be copied.

Installation and startup sound like pretty rough terrain, but with a couple of the right tools, you shouldn't have any trouble staying on the path. You may, however, see these signals along the way:

ERROR: Files could not be copied. Disk may be full.

You pushed the installation — you were running at bare minimum — and WordPerfect can't put any more files on the selected disk. Press any key and exit the installation procedure by pressing 9. After you free up more space on your hard disk, come back and do the install again. Keep in mind that some files may already have been copied, giving the illusion of less space.

Insufficient expanded or extended memory for /R

You've tried to start WordPerfect with the /RE, /R or /RX switch. WordPerfect is telling you that there's not enough high memory available to store the program files. If you are sure that you do have enough expanded memory and WordPerfect isn't seeing it, consult your witch doctor: your Expanded Memory Manager (EMS) may not be properly installed. You don't need to do anything to get around this error; WordPerfect will simply load the files conventionally.

Insufficient file handles, MINIMUM of FILES=25 required

You tried to start WordPerfect but the program found out that your FILES= line in CONFIG.SYS is set too low. Edit the line to FILES=30, save the file, and reboot your computer. When you try to start WordPerfect again, it will find the file handles it needs in order to run.

You Know You're Really in Trouble When . . .

Most installation and startup problems in WordPerfect aren't fatal. They *are* pretty annoying, though. You think someone should give you a medal just for trying to install this monster package, and now it's giving you fits.

Well, you suppose there's something to be said for being on dry ground finally, but you hadn't planned on taking another one of these see-the-world excursions again so soon. This is just the kind of unexpected detour that makes for the beginning of a good horror film.

You are out of disk storage space

No matter what you do, your 40MB hard drive just isn't going to give you the room that you need to install WordPerfect. If you've tried using a compression utility (like DoubleSpace in DOS 6.X) and cleaned everything off you can afford to remove, you're stuck unless you add another hard drive or replace the one you've got with a larger drive. Today, 210MB hard drives are pretty common, so if you're using a system with a 40MB hard drive, your computer is underpowered by most programs' standards. Shell out the extra resources (or get your boss to write the check) and add to your storage capabilities. You'll be glad you did.

One of your installation disks is bad

You keep getting errors when you insert one of the WordPerfect program disks. Are you using the original or a backup copy? If it's a backup, try the original and see whether the same error appears. If the disk is bad, contact WordPerfect Corporation at 800-228-9012. Be sure to have your software registration number handy.

Chapter 2

Sinister Setup

Paths through Peril

Sometimes survival is sheer drudgery. Find the fruit, wash the fruit, eat the fruit. Catch the crab, cook the crab, eat the crab. But let your mind wander for a moment, and — *ouch*! Who forgot to cook the crab?

Setting up WordPerfect involves adjusting those simple little things that can suddenly turn on you if you're not careful. You may, for example, find yourself with a keyboard with strange keys, a display that loses characters, or an erratic mouse.

WordPerfect, the Mouse Terror

Poison: Mouse faints at WP startup

You were just using the DOS shell, so you know that your mouse is working. But, suddenly, when you start WordPerfect, you have got no mouse.

Antidote: Press Shift-F1, 1 to display the Mouse settings. The first item, Type, shows the mouse driver WordPerfect sees for your system. Otherwise, press 1 to see a list of available mouse types. If you see your mouse on the list, you can select it. Press 2, Auto Select, to let WordPerfect choose a mouse driver for you.

If your mouse is still fainting after you return to the program, exit, reboot, and try again. Still no mouse? Call the witch doctor. Most likely, there's a battle of mouse drivers going on in the dark recesses of your system unit. It's ugly and it will give you nightmares. Better leave it to someone trained in computer mysticism.

Mouseractivity

Poison: Erratic mouse behavior

You've had your mouse a long time. You're kind of attached to it (and so is your computer). You've learned just how far to push north in order to get to the menu bar. You know just how fast to double-click. Dragging is a breeze.

But then you start using WordPerfect 6.0, and the personality of your mouse changes. It seems more ambitious. It wants to move faster. It makes you nervous.

Antidote: You can slow that little fellow down by pressing Shift-F1 and selecting Mouse. When the Mouse dialog box appears, slow down that Acceleration Factor by clicking on the down-pointing triangle. When you've got the Acceleration Factor where you want it, click on OK.

Terrific! Just what we need — a hurricane!

Give Me a Double (Click)

Poison: Dead double-click

You won't notice this problem until you start working with text. Say you decide that using the word *idiot* in your memo to the board of directors was a bit hasty — perhaps a more watered-down phrase would suffice. But when you attempt to select the word *idiot* — just point and double-click, right? — and the cursor just blinks back at you.

Where's the highlight? When you double-click, the word is supposed to highlight. That's one of the cardinal rules of word processing.

Antidote: Don't worry — it's probably not your mouse. If the mouse sees one click, it should see two. Display the Setup menu by pressing Shift-F1. Then press 1 to select the Mouse settings. If the Double-click interval is set to anything less than 50, increase it. You have to be an awful quick draw to get WordPerfect to see supersonic double-clicks.

Left-Out Lefties?

Poison: Mouse-handedness problems

Once again, we get that painful reminder that majority rules. You don't have your mouse stuck over on the right side of your keyboard, like everyone else in your office. Yours sits on the left side. And you don't get that double-click twitch in your index finger — instead, your middle finger is always aching by the end of the day.

A *driver* is a small instruction file your programs need in order to work with the various parts of your computer. For example, a mouse driver contains information about the mouse, and a graphics driver contains information about the graphics card.

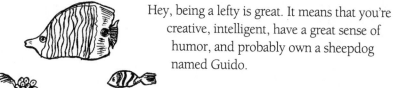

Hey, being a lefty is great. It means that you're creative, intelligent, have a great sense of humor, and probably own a sheepdog named Guido.

But most word processing programs don't stop to think about lefties, and you're tired of clicking in a right-handed world.

Antidote: Yes, Virginia, there is a Santa Claus. WordPerfect has an option — where are the trumpets? — that lets you set up your mouse for left-handed use. Press Shift-F1, 1, and 5. Then click on OK, rise to your feet, and give a salute in the general direction of Utah. And use your mouse proudly.

A Designated Graphics Driver

Poison: Nothing in the driver's seat

When you try to view the document in Graphics Mode, WordPerfect cheerfully reminds you

Serious about Setup? The setup options you select aren't written in stone: come back and change them whenever you like.

```
Graphics driver not
selected
```

What? Nobody said anything about a driver for graphics.

Antidote: A graphics driver gives WordPerfect important information about your monitor. And if you don't know much about your monitor, you can let WordPerfect make its own educated guess.

Open the File menu and choose Setup. Select Display, press 1, and then 1 again. When the Setup Graphics Screen Type dialog box appears, select 2 if you want WordPerfect to select the monitor type automatically, or you can choose the monitor that you want from the displayed list.

Failing the Driver's Test

Poison: Pulled over for bad driving

When you try to change to one of the alternate modes (like Graphics Mode or Page Mode), WordPerfect displays the rather ominous note

```
Driver Warning
```

What does that mean and what do you do about it?

Antidote: The graphics driver you installed isn't getting along with WordPerfect. In fact, WordPerfect is convinced that you chose the wrong driver.

How to fix? Choose another driver by pressing Shift-F1, selecting Display, and selecting 1. In the Setup Graphics Screen Type dialog box, choose either a different driver or 2, Auto Select, which lets WordPerfect go ahead and choose the driver that it thinks is best.

Graphics drivers WordPerfect needs in order to display correctly are stored in the WP60 directory. The display driver files end with the extension VRS. If you have trouble finding the graphics driver that you need, open the

Followed by one of the infamous earthquakes!

README.VRS file — a text file located in the WP60 directory, that gives you extra information about the WordPerfect graphics drivers.

Who Turned Out the Lights?

Poison: Peekaboo displays

You just started using WordPerfect and notice that you're leaning forward and squinting a lot. You can't really see much except the cursor and the highlighted letters in the menu names.

Antidote: This problem could be related to a number of things:

- *Is the brightness display on your monitor turned up?* (The brightness control should be on the side or front of your monitor.)

- *If you're using a laptop with an LCD display, is the sun shining on or near the screen?* (If so, try moving the laptop — tilting the screen may help — or choosing a darker room.)

- *If you've just installed WordPerfect, did you choose the right graphics driver?* (Find out by pressing Shift-F1 and selecting Display.)

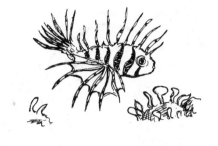

> *Could your color scheme be skewed?* (In the Display options, try selecting a different color.

Serious Screen Screwups

Poison: Flashing plaid displays

You started WordPerfect and it *sounded* like it loaded right. But the screen's — it's flashing all kinds of colors and plaid patterns.

Antidote: A display this fried isn't a good sign. Chances are, these symptoms indicate one of the following problems:

> *Your monitor cable may be loose.* Too easy, right? Check your cable connections to make sure.

> *Your graphics driver file could be missing or corrupted.* (You can't change the driver selected because you can't get into WordPerfect. But you can reinstall the program and choose a different graphics driver. Before you go to the trouble, though, ask the witch doctor for advice.)

> *Your graphics card may be loose or not functioning.* (You can check this possibility by rebooting. If DOS comes up legibly, the problem isn't your graphics card.)

> *Your computer may have caught a virus.* (Do you hear any strange sound effects, like a bomb dropping or a high whistle? If you suspect a computer virus, get the witch doctor, quickly — and implement some kind of virus protection plan for the future.)

Obnoxious Screen Colors

Poison: Clash of the colors

Who designed this screen, anyway? Somebody's been playing around with your WordPerfect setup. You're looking at a color scheme that makes you wince.

Antidote: You can change the screen colors by pressing Shift-F1 and then 2. The Display settings appear. To change the colors in Graphics Mode (which includes Page Mode and Print Preview), press 1. To change the colors in Text Mode, press 2. You can select one of WordPerfect's preset color schemes, or you can mix and match your own. (But be careful, some combinations are lethal.)

Auto-Backup or Bust

Poison: Soon isn't soon enough

Your local power company, Eccentric Electric, is having a supply and demand problem. The lights are wavering; your monitor is flickering. Now, what about those automatic backups?

And finally, one of those darned rockslides!

How to Make a Backup

If you work alone in a vacuum, you're probably on your own when it comes to backing up important files. If you are part of a network, you may have a system-wide backup procedure to follow (check with your witch doctor — or system administrator — to be sure).

If you are responsible for saving your own data, make sure that you back up your files regularly. The best solution to many potential file and disk problems is to whip out that backup copy and load the files back on the drive.

How do you make a backup? WordPerfect will make an automatic backup of your current file for you, depending on how you've set the Backup options in the Environment dialog box. The default is a backup of the current file every ten minutes.

But these backup precautions don't take care of your programs. Or all the rest of your important data, for that matter.

DOS has a BACKUP command that will create a safe copy of your files. But be prepared — it takes a lot of blank, formatted disks (about one per megabyte of storage space). After you back up the files by using BACKUP, you use the RESTORE command to return the files to your hard disk. With DOS 6, a new improved backup utility was introduced: MSBACKUP.

Where to Find a Good Witch Doctor

Even though you won't find a good witch doctor lounging behind every sand dune, you can find one if you look in the right places:

- Your company's technical support staff

- WordPerfect's phone support staff

- Professors who teach computer courses

- Knowledgeable computer salespeople

- On-line computer-related forums (some are sponsored by software or hardware manufacturers)

- The experienced coworker in the next cubicle

- In the Yellow Pages, under Computer Consultants

- Members of your local computer society or user groups

- Your friends, your parents, your neighbors, and your kids!

Antidote: When you first install WordPerfect, the program is set to back up your current files automatically every ten minutes. You can change that increment, if you want (but choose something practical). If the brownouts are happening every four minutes, set your backup timer to three (and then take one-minute breaks for yourself).

Unexpected Beeps

Poison: What do the beeps mean?

WordPerfect seems to beep at weird times. You are typing a document and get a beep. Later, when you get an error about the printer not being ready, no beep.

Antidote: You can control the events for the WordPerfect gong by displaying Setup (Shift-F1), Environment, and Beep Options (2). By default, WordPerfect beeps when it wants to know whether or not to hyphenate something. If you want, it will also beep when an error is encountered (logical) or when a search operation has turned up empty. Make your selection by clicking on the option(s) that you want and click on OK.

Techie Term

A *default* is a setting that is chosen automatically during installation. You can change defaults at any time to customize the way you work with Word-Perfect.

Not Inches, Centimeters!

Poison: Need different units for measurements

It's bad enough not having a ruler bar, and then, when you try to figure out the status line, you see

```
Doc 1 Page 1 Ln 1.17" Pos 2.2"
```

What's that? *Inches*? You don't work in inches.
The people in production want everything
measured in picas.

Antidote: You can change the way
WordPerfect shows its measurements by
getting to the Environment dialog box. Press
Shift-F1 and then 3. Now press 7, and the
Units of Measure dialog box appears. You need to change two options:
Display/Entry of Numbers and Status Line Display.

Both items have double-headed arrows at the end of the line. Put the
mouse pointer on the arrow and press and hold the mouse button. (If you
let up, the list disappears.) Drag the highlight to the option that you want
(in this case, picas) and release the mouse button.

It's that simple.

Remember to choose the setting that you want for both Display/Entry of
Numbers and Status Line Display. Changing one does not automatically
change the other. The *status line* on your screen tells you what document
you're viewing, what page you're on, and the current cursor position.

It's So Slooooowwww . . .

Poison: Sluggish typing

Some people can type without thinking. Most
people can think without typing. A few can do both.

If you're a 100-wpm person (and
proud of it), having a cursor that
lags behind the characters as you
type will drive you crazy. Your

fingers will be working on page 2 while WordPerfect plods along at the bottom of page 1.

Antidote: You can control WordPerfect's cursor speed so that it stays right with you as you move through a document. The default is 50 cps (that's characters per second), which is Superman fast, so if your computer is lagging, either you've got bionic fingers or someone has changed the cursor speed setting in your version of WordPerfect.

Press Shift-F1 and choose Environment. Then change Cursor Speed to the setting that you want and click on OK.

Note: If you like the cursor speed the way it is in your other programs — and in DOS — you can disable WordPerfect's cursor speed at startup by typing the command WP /nc when you begin.

Keyboard Kraziness

Poison: Unfamiliar keyboard turf

You're accustomed to the keyboard layout and function of WordPerfect 5.1, and this new version messes you up. Your fingers are stumbling all over each other. The new template is giving you nightmares.

Antidote: Knowing that such a major change would unsettle some die-hard 5.1 fans, WordPerfect 6.0 includes several options for those who prefer the good old days. In Setup Environment, you can choose the WordPerfect 5.1 keyboard by typing K and select the 5.1 cursor movement functions by typing W. (You can disable the 5.1 keyboard by pressing F1 during your work session. That returns the normal 6.0 keyboard functions.)

Everywhere a Macro, Macro

Poison: No room on the keys

You want to try adding your own macro, but to which key? They are all used for something or other (just look at that template!).

Antidote: Lucky for you, WordPerfect 6.0 has built-in swappable keyboards. No, that doesn't mean that you unplug your keyboard and plug another in. It means that WordPerfect can change the way that the keys do things, depending on what keyboard file you have loaded.

When you start WordPerfect, the [ORIGINAL] keyboard is loaded. That's the default for 6.0. There's also a WordPerfect for Windows 5.2 keyboard

Words of Wisdom:

Environment Settings

From the name, you may have trouble telling what the Environment settings do. (Hint: It has nothing to do with clean air.) Environment settings control backup and beep options, cursor speed, the Undo feature, the selected unit of measure, and other arcane settings like Language, Delimited Text Options, and Hyphenation prompting.

Button Bars

Button bars are on-screen buttons you can use to select often-used commands with a click of a mouse. You can choose from WordPerfect's seven preset button bars or create your own. You can, for example, use one button bar when formatting a document and another when editing text.

(CUAWPW52), a MACROS keyboard (with 6.0 macros plugged in), and an EQUATION keyboard (for using the Equation Editor).

Note: Before you modify a keyboard file, make sure that you make a copy of it and give it a unique name. If you change the original keyboards and later want the files back, you'll have to get them off your original WordPerfect disks.

Who Broke the Keyboard?

Poison: Malfunctioning keys

You press Alt and the highlighted letter to open the menu. Nothing happens. You've checked all of the keys, and none of them are stuck try another letter and get some error about a missing macro file. All you want to do is open the Help menu.

Antidote: Press Shift-F1 to display the Setup menu. Chances are, the wrong keyboard is selected. Press 4 and check the keyboard files. Is ORIGINAL chosen? If not, click on it and click on OK. If ORIGINAL was chosen and you were still having trouble with what should be routine key combinations, give your witch doctor a call. Your keyboard file may be corrupted — or at least edited by an unfriendly sort.

Where Is Everything?

Poison: A naked screen

This is a *new* program? This is the one everyone says is so *helpful*? Where are all the windows? What about buttons? You want some help, darn it. All you see is a single strip across the top of the screen and some gibberish at the bottom.

Antidote: Open the View menu and click on Ribbon. The Ribbon gives you information about the document that you're creating: how many columns, what text alignment is chosen, what font is being used, and so on.

Now open the View menu and choose Button Bar. The Button Bar that you see is the default. It gives you an easy way to save, print, preview, and display a file in Graphics Mode.

And the gibberish in the bottom right corner of the screen *is* gibberish, pretty much. It tells you what document number you're looking at (you can have up to nine documents open in WP6), what page, what line, and the amount of space from the left margin. There may be a time when you are glad you have that information.

Screen Overload

Poison: Cluttered screen

You've got so much stuff on your screen you can't believe it. You've got menu bars and button bars and outline bars and scroll bars. Enough bars to keep a college student busy for a month.

All you want to do is type some text. Where's that old Smith-Corona?

Antidote: Wait — before you give up and go back to the typewriter, try this: press Ctrl-F3 and then Shift-F1 (or view, screen, setup). Remove the X from in front of all the screen elements that are bothering you. For a bare-bones display, uncheck everything except Pull-Down Menus.

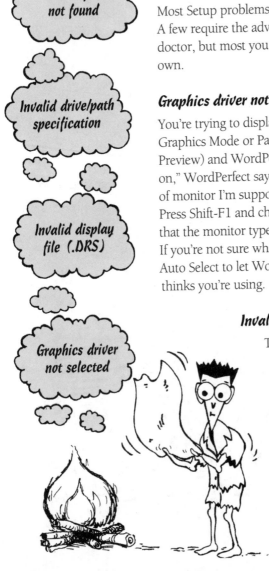

Reading Smoke Signals

Most Setup problems are relatively easy to fix. A few require the advice of a good witch doctor, but most you can decipher on your own.

Graphics driver not selected

You're trying to display the document in Graphics Mode or Page Mode (or even Print Preview) and WordPerfect is unwilling. "Hold on," WordPerfect says, "and tell me what kind of monitor I'm supposed to be displaying." Press Shift-F1 and choose Display. Make sure that the monitor type you're using is selected. If you're not sure what you've got, choose Auto Select to let WordPerfect choose what it thinks you're using.

Invalid display file (.DRS)

The .DRS file WordPerfect needs in order to display your files has either been changed or damaged. If you feel like rolling up your shirtsleeves, get your backup copies of your original program disks and reinstall the .DRS file that's giving

WordPerfect trouble. If you'd rather play it safe, ask the witch doctor for advice before proceeding.

Invalid drive/path specification

You may see this error while setting up the location of your files in the Setup menu if you enter a directory name that doesn't exist. Check your entry and make any corrections before you click on OK.

Macro file not found

You may not expect to see this strange error as you're working. But if the MACRO keyboard is selected and you press a key combination that doesn't do anything, WordPerfect is going to go looking for that macro file. Just press Esc to get past the error message (and change your keyboard back to normal by pressing Shift-F1, 4, and choosing ORIGINAL).

You Know You're Really in Trouble When . . .

You delete the WPC6DOS directory

You're cleaning off your hard disk to make more room for your WordPerfect files and you see — what's this? — a WPC6DOS subdirectory. Well, there's your WP60 directory over there, so this directory couldn't be part of WordPerfect. Wrong. Because WPC6DOS is stored off the root directory (probably C:\), you may not realize that it's part of WordPerfect. If you delete the files stored there, it's reinstall time.

You can't find WordPerfect in Windows.

You know you installed it, where did it go? If you plan to run WordPerfect for DOS as a DOS application within Windows, you'll need to set up a special icon for it. Call your witch doctor for assistance.

Chapter 3

Text Terrors

Paths through Peril

Entering text is the easy part, right? On WordPerfect Island, there's only one hard and fast rule: expect the unexpected.

Someone should have warned you about the rain forest. Who knows what terrifying creatures may be lurking up in the canopy. All you need now is to have

some boa constrictors dropping down on you, or almost worse yet — these awful blood-sucking leaches. Besides, it'll probably be this gagging humidity that will kill you finally anyway.

Rollover Typeover

Poison: Runaway characters

Your assistant finished entering the notes from the recent Board of Directors meeting. Now you've got to turn those notes into some kind of report for your boss. You open the file — ah, there it is — and start typing away. As you type, your characters roll right over the text that was already there.

Antidote: First, stop typing. Next, look in the bottom left corner of the screen. There's probably a little message that says Typeover, which means Typeover mode is in effect. What can you do?

➧ *Press Ctrl-Z (that's Undo).* If you're lucky, this action will restore the text. If you've been typing for a while without paying attention, however, you may not be able to restore much of the typed-over material.

➧ *Open the File menu and choose Save As.* When the dialog box appears, enter a new name for the file and press Enter. That saves your changes (so that you can keep the good ones) in one file and preserves your assistant's file as it was before you changed it.

➧ *If you selected the Back Up Original Document (.BK!) on Save or Exit option in the Environment, Backup setup options box, you may be able to open the backup file that WordPerfect made.* The file will have the same root name as your current document, but the extension will be .BK!.

Note: For more about finding and working with files, see Chapter 4.

There's More Than One Way to Block Text

Poison: Mouseless blocking

Due to circumstances beyond your control, you find yourself temporarily mouseless. Perhaps the little guy got all gummed up inside, and now you

Words of Wisdom:

Typeover and Insert Modes

WordPerfect has two text-entry modes: Typeover and Insert. Insert is the default, causing the characters that you type to be inserted at the cursor position, pushing all other characters to the right. When you select Typeover (by purposely or accidentally pressing the Insert key), the characters that you type replace any characters already there.

View Modes

WordPerfect 6.0 is much more fun to look at than its predecessor. Now you've got a choice — Text Mode (for text), Graphics Mode (which shows text and graphics), and Page Mode (which shows the text and special layout items such as headers, footers, and footnotes). For Page Mode disturbances, see Chapter 5. For Graphics Mode goof-ups, see Chapter 7. (Text Mode issues are explained in this chapter. But you knew that, right?)

Function Key Commands

WordPerfect is a function-key-heavy program. You'll find a function-key command for almost every operation possible. Each function key has four functions: one when pressed alone, one when pressed with Shift, one when pressed with Ctrl, and one when pressed with Alt. For example, F1 gets Help; Shift-F1 displays the Setup dialog box; Ctrl-F1 brings the Writing Tools menu to the screen; Alt-F1 pops up the WordPerfect Shell. For help in deciphering these multitalented key combinations, see your WordPerfect template or use the handy Function Key Reference Card in your copy of *WordPerfect For Dummies* by Dan Gookin.

have to wait while the witch doctor finds you a new mouse. But in the meantime, you've still got to get this report done. And you can't even figure out how to highlight text without your mouse.

Antidote: Highlighting text will seem like a lot of trouble when you're using the keyboard, but it can be done. Put the cursor where you want the block to begin; press Alt-F4 (or open the Edit menu and choose Block). Use the arrow keys to highlight the text that you want to block. Now you can proceed with your editing tasks.

Hold-On Blocking

Poison: Cancel that highlight!

You've just highlighted an area that you didn't mean to highlight. When you pressed the arrow keys, you just expanded the highlight. How do you get rid of the thing?

Antidote: To cancel a text section that you've marked as a block, press Esc or F7. If you're using the mouse, click outside the highlighted area.

Page-Break Panic

Poison: Uncontrollable breaks

The managers were very specific about what information is supposed to go on what sheet of the schedule. You've been moving things around in your document all morning, trying to get the items to fit the way they asked you to. Right before you're ready to print, you notice a page break line in a really bad place.

Antidote: A soft page break, which looks like a single line, is inserted automatically when a certain number of lines have been entered on one page. You can't delete a soft page break.

You can, however, force a hard page break where you want the new page to begin. If, for example, the page break occurs just after a heading and you want the page to break before the heading, move the cursor up to the line preceding the heading and press Ctrl-Enter. This command forces a hard page break (which looks like a double line). You can delete hard page breaks if necessary. Keep in mind that headers and footers reduce the lines per page available for text.

Building on the Block

Poison: Not-done-yet blocking

You've already selected the section that you want to copy and then — oops, there's another part you missed. How can you select the additional text without letting go of the text that you've already blocked?

Antidote: You can add another section to your text block by pressing Shift and clicking in the other section. Everything between the beginning point of the block and the point that you just clicked is highlighted. This method only works if your are extending from the endpoint of the block.

Ribbon Troubles

Poison: Keyboard doesn't work

It's great to have the button bars and the ribbon right here on-screen where you can get to them easily. But when you try to use the arrow keys up to the ribbon to select something, the keyboard doesn't respond.

Antidote: The ribbon is designed specifically for use with the mouse. Notice that there are no hot keys (no underlined or bold keys) that you can press to select items on the ribbon.

To use the ribbon, point to the setting that you want to select and click.

Undo Doesn't

Poison: Hey! I needed that!

It's easy to get confused when you're cutting and pasting text. You move this paragraph to that position and that paragraph to the other position and — hey — where did that paragraph go?

Antidote: You may be expecting too much. Undo, in fact, pales in comparison to Undelete, which at least gives you your last three erroneous deletions. Undo just undoes whatever you just did (try saying that three times fast). So if you just backspaced through a word, Undo returns it. But what about that number you moved from that page to this one? Undo will remove the number from its new spot but won't put the number back in it's original place.

Escape Doesn't, Either

Poison: Lemme go!

When you press Esc to back out of an operation, WordPerfect offers up the word that you deleted three pages ago. You don't want a *word*; you want to cancel Graphics Mode and return to Text Mode.

Antidote: First of all, you can't cancel Graphics Mode by pressing Esc. (In other programs, you can switch from a preview mode to normal mode by pressing Esc, but not here.) The key for switching modes is Ctrl-F3.

What's more, just because WordPerfect went through an upgrade, don't expect it to go completely conventional. WordPerfect 5.1 used the F1 key to cancel operations; in WordPerfect 6.0, it's F7. (F1 is now Help.) The Esc key is now the "Give-me-that-back-I-didn't-mean-to-delete-it" key.

Dead-End Undelete

Poison: Uh-oh deletions

It's late in the afternoon and your mind is beginning to wander toward dinner. You glance back at the screen just as — what? — you didn't delete that, did you?

Antidote: Whether your goose is cooked will depend on several things:

- *Was the deletion less than three removals ago?* (If so, you may be able to restore the text with Undelete. Press Esc and if you don't see the text that you need, select Previous Deletion. Repeat this step until you've seen the last three items that you deleted.)

- *Did you save the file before you made those changes?*

- *Did you turn on the backup feature in the Environment options dialog box?* If you did, the file is saved in the WPDOCS directory with the .BK! extension.

- *Do you have cookies in your desk to feed the witch doctor?*

Clipboard Keeper

Poison: Need clipboard contents

You want to move around a few blocks of text, but the information that you've got on the clipboard is really important.

Antidote: You can do several things:

- *If you started from the WordPerfect Shell, open the Edit menu and choose Append.* From the submenu, select To Clipboard. This procedure adds the new text to the old text on the clipboard. (You may not want it mixed together, but at least you've got both sections intact.)

- *Again, if you started from the Shell, you can use Go to Shell (in the File menu) to display the Shell dialog box.* The Clipboard number lists the clipboard on which the important information is already stored. You can change the number — to anything from 1 to 79 — to start putting items on a new clipboard and preserve the contents of the old.

- *If the information is really important, save it as a file.* Or open a new file (use New in the File menu) and paste the data in the new document window. You can have up to nine open documents in WordPerfect 6.0. Remember the save function with a block hilighted with a block will save just the block.

Techie Term

A *style* is a preset format that you can apply to text in your document. You can create your own styles for text formats that you use often and save the styles in a *style library*.

Dancing Text

Poison: Mysterious moves

You were just typing happily along, minding your own business, when suddenly your text indented itself.

Antidote: Ask yourself these things:

- *Did you press the Indent key (F4) without knowing it?*

- *Did you move or delete a code?* Look in Reveal Codes to see. Position the cursor on the spot where everything changed and press Alt-F3.

- *Did you choose an open style?* An open style changes all text from the cursor point on.

- *Did you block the text before you began?* Blocking text automatically marks the beginning and ending points for the style. Without the end point, the style is applied to all remaining text.

Note: For more information about blocking and applying style and alignment options to text, see *WordPerfect 6 For Dummies*, by Dan Gookin.

How to Create a Style Library

Styles are witch-doctor-like tools because they help you work smarter instead of harder. Are you always highlighting text and selecting the same format options? Do you tend to repeat the same font or style? You can assign those things to a style that you then apply to your text, thus allowing WordPerfect to take care of the fonts and formats for you.

To create your own library of styles, start with your current document. Create the styles that you want and then press Alt-F8. The Style List dialog box appears. Click Save at the bottom of the screen and enter the path and file name for the style library in the Personal: line. (To help you remember that this file stores your styles, use .STY as the file's extension.) If you want to include WordPerfect's preset styles in your new style library, click Save WP System Styles. Then click OK.

When you want to use the style library with a document, click Options in the Style List box; then enter the name of the Personal or Shared Library that you want to use. If you enter a library name that has not been created yet, WordPerfect creates the file, and you can add styles to it as you go along.

For best results, remember to save a copy of the style library along with any files that you save on disk. That way, if you go to retrieve the files later, the files will still have access to their styles, and they should appear with the right font and format.

What Information to Have Ready for the Witch Doctor

Before you talk about your specific problem, the witch doctor may ask you for some of the following information. If you're prepared, you'll be able to get on with the fix much more quickly.

- What is the version number and release date of WP.EXE? (Open the Help menu and choose WP Info to find out.)

- What kind of system are you using (brand name and model)?

- What DOS version do you use? (Not sure? Exit to DOS, type VER, and write down what you see.)

- What monitor and graphics card do you have (brand name and model)?

- Are you using a network or stand-alone machine?

- Do you have a printed copy of WPINFO.EXE? (See the Chapter 1 sidebar, "How to Make a System Info Report," for specific instructions.)

- What is your name, department number, software serial number, computer warranty expiration date, purchase date, and other identifying information?

- Do you have any special peripherals hooked up to your machine?

Short-Sheeted Reveal Codes

Poison: Too-small display

You're supposed to make sense out of four lines of strange-looking characters at the bottom of your screen? You pressed Alt-F3 to Reveal Codes, but you can only see a couple of words from your document.

Antidote: A larger screen area will help. Change the amount of the screen given over to Reveal Codes by pressing Ctrl-F3 and increasing the Reveal Codes Windows Percentage. For most operations, having Reveal Codes set to 40 or 50 percent is fine. For documents with only a few run-of-the-mill codes, you may want to decrease the percentage to give you more room for the document view.

It's All Greek to Me!

Poison: Unreadable codes

You know how to display Reveal Codes, but how can you know what the various codes do? They are all three letter abbreviations from the language of some strange lost continent.

Antidote: You can get WordPerfect to give you the long version of the code names by pressing Ctrl-F3 and then Shift-F1 to display the Screen Setup dialog box. Then click Display Details in the Reveal Codes options. For example, [Bookmark] turns into [Bookmark:QuickMark], telling you that you used a quickmark and not a special symbol to mark your place in the document.

Search and Destroy

Poison: Over-centering

You thought that they wanted you to center all the subheads in your research paper. But you just received your first draft back and there are red marks all over it, shouting "Left align! Left align!" Is there any way to go through the entire document and remove all those [Center] codes without looking for them one by one?

Antidote: Use WordPerfect's search-and-replace feature. Open the Edit menu and choose Replace. Click Specific Codes and choose Just (for Justification) from the displayed list. A pop-up box appears, asking you to choose the justification type. In this case, choose Center. Then click Search and Delete or press F4. WordPerfect returns all your centered heads to left-justified text.

Hint: Use a style, and then just edit the style. It updates the document.

Quick, Comments, Hide!

Poison: Incriminating comments

You've put notes to yourself in the first draft of your report. Now your boss wants to see the draft, but you don't want him to see the notes.

Antidote: If you entered the notes as regular text, you can convert the text to comments and then hide them. Highlight the text that you want to hide. Press Ctrl-F7 to display the Notes box. Then choose Comment and Create.

Words of Wisdom:

Bookmarks

A bookmark marks your place in your WordPerfect document so that when you return to the file, you can pick right up where you left off. Set a bookmark by putting the cursor where you want it and pressing Ctrl-Q. Find the bookmark later with Ctrl-F.

Sound Clips

WordPerfect 6.0 adds a special multimedia feature — sound clips — to its range of possibilities. If your computer has a sound board, you can add voice-over notes, sound effects, and even music to your documents. To set up WordPerfect's sound capabilities, press Ctrl-F7. (For more about wrestling with WordPerfect's sound potential, see Chapter 7.)

These steps turn the text into a Comment which is shown on your document in a rectangular box.

Now hide the comment by choosing Screen Setup (Ctrl-F3) and making sure that Display Comments (in Windows Options) is unchecked. (It is usually checked by default.) When you return to the document, your comment is still there, but the only evidence is the [Comment] code in the Reveal Codes screen. To redisplay the comment, return to Screen Setup and check the Display Comments check box.

Of course, another option would be to use the Sound Clips feature to create voice messages instead of leaving notes lying around.

Comments don't print, even if they show in the box.

Out-to-Lunch Speller

Poison: Stolen dictionary

You need to spell check your document in the worst way. (Or you want to check it because you spell in the worst way.) But when you open the Tools menu, choose Writing Tools, and start the Speller, WordPerfect tells you that it can't find the dictionary file it needs.

Antidote: This message comes to you in the form of a dialog box, and WordPerfect waits patiently while you fight the panic and look frantically for the missing file. WordPerfect needs WPUS.LEX (the US is for United States, so if you're using a different language, your letters might be different) in order to check your spelling.

Use the Directory Tree to look for the file. If the file is present, try running the Speller again. If you get the same

error, or the file isn't where it should be, give the witch doctor a call. You'll be able to get the original WPUS.LEX off your WordPerfect program disks — unless the file on the originals is corrupted, too (and in that case, it's time for a nice, long lunch).

No-Way Thesaurus

Poison: Disabled Thesaurus

You double-click the word that you want to check and open the Tools menu. You then choose Writing Tools and the various WordPerfect writing assistants pop up. You click Thesaurus and nothing happens.

Antidote: If you don't get an error and WordPerfect just sits there after you click Thesaurus, the Thesaurus files have not been installed. You can update the install if you've got the original program disks (but ask your witch doctor before proceeding).

Feeling that Grammatik Strain

Poison: Memory drain

You get ready to check the document that you've been working on all afternoon. You display the Writing Tools and choose Grammatik. After a moment, the Grammatik 5 opening menu appears. But that's followed by a message that Grammatik can't go any farther. Not enough RAM.

Antidote: Grammatik isn't a tiny little thing that just pops up when you want it to. It's a full-blown program with lots of features that may or may not fit into your available RAM.

🖱 If you started WordPerfect by using the Shell, don't run Grammatik from within WordPerfect. Exit to the Shell and run Grammatik from there to save some space.

🖱 If you aren't using the Shell, exit to DOS and try running Grammatik in the WPC60DOS directory by typing GMK and pressing Enter.

Grammatik Killed My Mouse!

Poison: No-pulse mousie

Like you don't have enough to worry about. The managers are going to read your document and rip it to shreds. You've been asking everyone to proofread it for you. People are dodging into stairwells when they see you coming. Finally someone put a Post-It note on your monitor: *Use Grammatik!* You looked it up, started the program, and now your mouse is dead.

Antidote: Grammatik is an add-on program that WordPerfect kindly bundles in so that you can add that extra oomph! to your writing. (Or, at least, to keep you from being an editor's lunch.) But because Grammatik is an add-on, or third-party, program (meaning someone else developed it), it doesn't use your WordPerfect mouse drivers. So your mouse may work in WordPerfect, but when you use Grammatik, it may not.

Don't worry — this problem's not fatal (to you or to the mouse). Just make sure that MOUSE.COM is loaded before you start Grammatik. In most cases, MOUSE.COM is run in your AUTOEXEC.BAT file, but if it's not, you can change to your MOUSE directory (it may be called something else on your machine — use DOS's DIR /W command to find it) and type MOUSE to load the necessary driver.

Reading Smoke Signals

If all you're doing in WordPerfect is simple typing — nothing fancy, like spelling checkers or thesaurus or grammar checkers — you won't have much to look at in the way of smoke signals.

Dictionary File Not Found

You are trying to run the speller and the primary spelling dictionary, WPUS.LEX, isn't where it should be. Use the Directory Tree to search the WPC60DOS directory. If the file is missing, ask the witch doctor to help you retrieve it from the original program disks. If the file is where it's supposed to be, it's probably damaged, which means that you'll still need the witch doctor and his magic expanding-file trick.

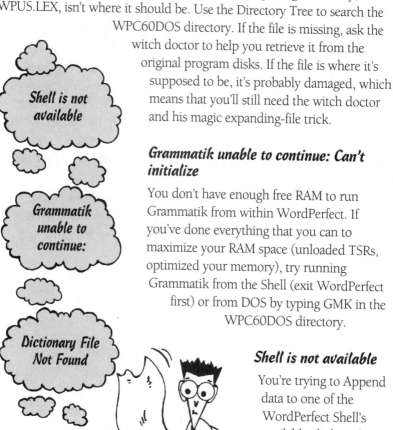

Grammatik unable to continue: Can't initialize

You don't have enough free RAM to run Grammatik from within WordPerfect. If you've done everything that you can to maximize your RAM space (unloaded TSRs, optimized your memory), try running Grammatik from the Shell (exit WordPerfect first) or from DOS by typing GMK in the WPC60DOS directory.

Shell is not available

You're trying to Append data to one of the WordPerfect Shell's available clipboards, but you haven't started the Shell. Save your file, exit to DOS, and change to the WPC60DOS directory by typing CD \WPC60DOS and pressing Enter. Now type SHELL and press Enter. After the Shell comes up, you can start WordPerfect and open your file as usual.

You Know You're in Trouble When . . .

You accidentally searched for a phrase and replaced it with nothing

When you ask WordPerfect to perform this task, it looks for every occurrence of the search text, wipes it away, and leaves nothing in its place — which could make for some pretty holey documents. You have a couple of good cures for this mistake if you catch it quickly: abandon the file without saving your changes (of course, anything else you've done since the last save will be lost, too), or close the file and open a backup copy (one that you made yourself or one that WordPerfect made with the .BK! extension).

You click on the down-arrow beside the font list and your font isn't on the list.

Try typing the name of the font in the font text box that appears above the list. WordPerfect will search for the font that you specify. If WordPerfect does not locate the font, make sure that the font has been installed properly.

Chapter 4

File Floundering

Paths through Peril

Working with files can be as slippery as trying to catch fish with your bare hands. Unless you've got your angle, timing, and pressure right, you're going to come up with a bunch of nothing. Maybe you could make better use of your resources . . . where's that spear?

My New File Is Gone!

Poison: Here-again, gone-again files

You were just working on it. You saved and exited right before lunch and now here you are, fileless. Where could it be?

Antidote: First, walk back through the steps that you took to find the file. You should begin with the Open command in the File menu. When the Open Document box appears, click the down-arrow at the end of the Filename: line. Your most recently worked-on document should be there (the drop-down list shows the last four files that you've created and/or modified).

Which File Is Which?

Poison: File amnesia

Put one hundred files in the same directory, with their eight-character file names and three-character extensions, and they are all basically going to look alike. If you've named them things like MEMO101.DOC and REP123.DOC, you're going to have trouble remembering what's in them. How can you find that one file that you've got to have *fast*?

Antidote: Display the File Manager by opening the File menu and choosing the File Manager command. When the dialog box appears, choose the drive and directory that you want to display. Now, in the file list, highlight one of the files that you're wondering about and select Look. WordPerfect gives you a peek at the file but won't let you touch. Scroll through, and if you're convinced that it's the one you want, click Close. Back at the File Manager, open the file by choosing Open into New Document.

Will the Real File Please Stand Up?

Poison: Up-close file inspection

You've been working on this report for days. You took it home last night and worked after you were able to get the kids to relinquish the mouse. You brought the report back and loaded it on your machine. You changed the file name slightly so that it wouldn't overwrite the original, but now you can't remember which one is which. How can you find out which copy of the file is the most current?

Antidote: Select the File Manager by pressing F5 and use the Directory Tree to display the files in question. Look at the dates and times that the files were last updated. The most recent file should be the most current.

If for some reason the dates and times aren't working properly on your machine, you can use Compare Documents to find the changes. This command goes through the document that you choose and compares by word, phrase, sentence, or paragraph to isolate the changes. Any text that has been added appears in redline; deleted text is shown in strikeout. Click OK to start the compare procedure.

Old Files Just Fade Away

Poison: Trouble locating files

Now that you're accumulating a pretty hefty file library, you're having trouble finding files. How can you get a file when it *isn't* one of the last four you worked on?

WordPerfect's Friendly File Formats

Whether you're importing a file or exporting one, WordPerfect gets along well with the following programs and file formats: Ami Pro, ASCII, DisplayWrite, DOS Delimited Text, DCA, Microsoft Word, Word for Windows, RTF, earlier WordPerfect versions, and WordStar.

Antidote: Click on the File Manager and choose the Directory Tree. Go to the drive and directory that you want and click the mouse button. If you find yourself going to the same drive and directory time and time again, you may want to create a QuickList (see sidebar in this section).

☀ Words of Wisdom:

QuickList

You create a QuickList as a kind of WordPerfect shortcut to getting to directories or files that you use most often. Create a QuickList from the File Manager and specify the directory or file name so that you can move right to that location instead of going through all the ordinary hoopla of clicking buttons and making option choices.

ConvertPerfect

Having trouble converting the files that you need? ConvertPerfect may be able to help you. Start it from the Shell (from the WPC60DOS directory, type **Shell** and press Enter) and follow the on-screen prompts. Yes, it's more confusing than WordPerfect, but no one said file conversion would be *easy*.

How to Manage Your Files and Directories

WordPerfect gives you many ways to find and hold on to your files. You can locate the directory that you want by typing it in the Filename box, by clicking the File Manager's Directory Tree, or by creating a QuickList.

Think carefully about how you want the directories set up on your system. WordPerfect automatically creates a document directory — WPDOCS — into which all your documents are placed by default. But if every document you ever create goes into that directory, it's going to be pretty full in a short amount of time. You may want to consider other directories, perhaps organized by project name (NEWSLTRS, REPORTS, PRCOPY), by project type (EDITING, WRITING, INDEXING), or by client (ADDMORE, PHILIPS, WESTIN).

To create a new directory, display the File Manager screen and choose Change Default Dir. Type the name for the new directory and press Enter. When Word-Perfect asks you for confirmation, select Yes. (If you prefer, you can create the directory from DOS by using the MD command.)

But before you go creating directories all over your hard disk, ask the witch doctor for some hard-won advice on the best organizational strategies. You may find a few helpful tips that will prove worth their weight in gold over time.

What Stuff to Have Ready for the Witch Doctor

When the witch doctor arrives and sees that you have the contents of your satchel all ready for him, he will be pleased. Not to mention the fact that he might even be equipped now to solve your problem. All of these items that you have been collecting on your journey and carrying around with you are finally going to pay off:

- A written copy of any error messages that you received
- Printouts of your CONFIG.SYS and AUTOEXEC.BAT files
- Notes you made about the problem
- MSD printout from your system
- Printouts of important directories
- Your system disk and your startup disk
- Backups of files, if applicable
- Application master disks, if applicable
- The manuals for your hardware and software
- Any third-party books you have on the topic
- A bag of snack food (always applicable)

Hanging Out in the Margin

Poison: Runaway text

You were able to import the document from another word processor. But the file came in with a weird right margin. Each line extends out past the edge of the screen.

Antidote: First, take a look at the document in Graphics mode to make sure that things really are screwy. It may be that the file imported in a proportional font, and in Text mode the word wrap doesn't appear to be working. If things still look bad in Graphics mode, place the cursor immediately in front of the first paragraph and change the right margin by using Layout, Margins, and entering a higher value for the right margin.

Unsupported File Type

Poison: File format not recognized

You thought you'd save some time by getting your old word processing files and pulling the documents into WordPerfect. But when you select Open and choose the file on disk, WordPerfect tells you that it doesn't recognize the type and displays a list for you to choose the program that it was created in. Just one problem: your software isn't on the list.

Antidote: If there is another version of the program listed, try selecting the next closest version to yours. If WordPerfect still doesn't do the job, you can try ConvertPerfect, a utility included with WordPerfect (but run from the Shell) that converts files from popular programs to WordPerfect-likeable text. As a last resort, consider opening the documents in your other program and then saving them in a format that WordPerfect *will* recognize.

Even if you go ahead and export the files in a WordPerfect-compatible format, take a minute or two and contact WordPerfect for a conversion utility for your particular program.

Note: WordPerfect Corporation has a forum on CompuServe on which various updated drivers and conversion utilities are made available. Users can download the files at no charge (other than CompuServe charges and phone time) from the WordPerfect forum.

It Is Too There!

Poison: Invisible files

When you try to open a file on disk, WordPerfect doesn't show the file in any file list. Apparently, WordPerfect doesn't even know that the file exists.

Antidote: This problem could be one of several things:

➤ *Is the file type recognized by Word-Perfect?* Check your manual for a list of

recognized formats or read through the list in the File Format dialog box (displayed when you are importing a file).

➤ *Did you use the Directory Tree to scan the drive?* After you choose Open, click the File Manager button in the Open Document dialog box or press F5. Click Directory Tree or press F8. Now choose Other Drive. Select the drive where the files are stored and choose Rescan Drive to make sure that WordPerfect is seeing what's there.

➤ *Did you choose the right directory?* If you saved the file in a subdirectory of the disk, you may need to change directories before the file is displayed. Click the directory name (or the Parent name, if the subdirectory is currently displayed) to see more files.

🔊 *Did you use Name Search?* Pressing F2 to start Name Search is particularly helpful when you have many files to wade through in order to find the one that you need. But Name Search doesn't cross directories, though, so you must make sure that you're in the right place before you select it.

Asking for ASCII?

Poison: No extra space

You just opened this ASCII file and it came in better than everyone said it would. "Oh, you don't want to do *that*," they all said. "It's a hard-carriage-return nightmare." But because WordPerfect includes an option that takes care of carriage returns for you, your problem was something different: all the lines between paragraphs have been removed and your document looks like one huge paragraph.

Antidote: A trusty search-and-replace will solve this problem. Open the Edit menu and choose Replace. In the Search For: box, type a period (.) and press F5 to display Codes. Move the highlight to HRt and press Enter. Now press Tab to move to Replace With: and enter period (.)[HRt][HRt]. Then click Replace. See? An extra line with just a few keystrokes.

Techie Term

ASCII is an acronym for American Standard Code for Information Interchange, and it is a basic-level code that can be read and written by most programs. When you import an ASCII file, you won't see great formatting and fancy fonts, but you will, at least, see your text.

Hitting the Links?

Poison: Hypertext problems

This Hypertext thing sounds like space-age word processing, so you gave it a shot. After several blunt messages, you finally realize that WordPerfect wants you to add a bookmark or something.

Antidote: The basic process is as follows: create a bookmark here, create a bookmark there (in the current document or another one), and then link the two bookmarks. Or, if you prefer, you can have Hypertext run a macro.

(And that's a whole different book — *InfoWorld WordPerfect 6 SECRETS*, to be exact.)

The Bookmark Didn't Take

Poison: No-stick bookmark

You went through the process of creating a bookmark and it appeared to go well. But when you tried to create a hypertext link, you got a message saying that the bookmark wasn't found.

Antidote: When you are ready to create a Bookmark, either highlight the word at the cursor position to use as a bookmark name or type in a name of your own choosing. If you leave the default selection (which is the entire line of text), WordPerfect won't record the bookmark (even though it acts like it does).

I've Lost My Link to Reality

Poison: Next link, please

You've set up a link to take you to another document. But when you choose Jump/Run, WordPerfect tells you that the document isn't there.

Antidote: Click OK to get by the error message and then use the File Manager to double-check the path that you specified. Look carefully at the directory name and file name to make sure that you've got it right. If those things look OK, open the document and check the bookmark in the file. You can find out what bookmarks you've created by choosing Bookmark from the Edit menu. If you need to make changes, open the Tools menu, select Hypertext, and choose Edit Hypertext link; then make your changes.

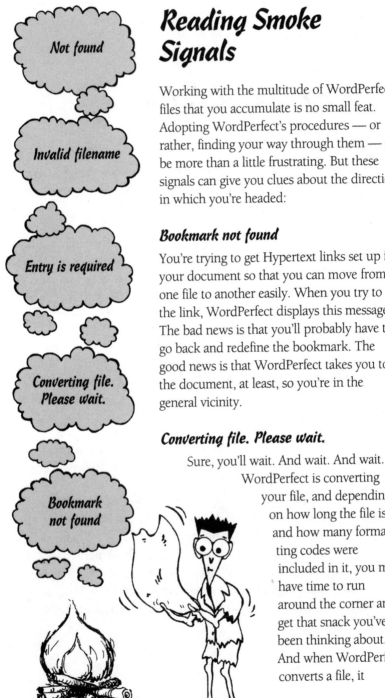

Reading Smoke Signals

Working with the multitude of WordPerfect files that you accumulate is no small feat. Adopting WordPerfect's procedures — or rather, finding your way through them — can be more than a little frustrating. But these signals can give you clues about the direction in which you're headed:

Bookmark not found

You're trying to get Hypertext links set up in your document so that you can move from one file to another easily. When you try to use the link, WordPerfect displays this message. The bad news is that you'll probably have to go back and redefine the bookmark. The good news is that WordPerfect takes you to the document, at least, so you're in the general vicinity.

Converting file. Please wait.

Sure, you'll wait. And wait. And wait. WordPerfect is converting your file, and depending on how long the file is and how many format-ting codes were included in it, you may have time to run around the corner and get that snack you've been thinking about. And when WordPerfect converts a file, it converts the file. So when you see the document on your screen, you know it's in 6.0 format.

Entry is required

This is a tight-mouthed message about HyperText links. You're trying to create a link and WordPerfect is trying to tell you that you've skipped creating a bookmark (which is used to anchor one end of the link). Click OK to get around the message, click Cancel, and create your bookmark in the file before attempting Hypertext again.

Invalid filename

Yes, we told you to be descriptive with your filenames. However, if you name a file with one of the extensions reserved by DOS, you'll see this sort of error in WordPerfect. As a general rule, stay away from these extensions: CON, AUX, NUL, and PRN.

Not found

This nondescript little message appears when you're trying to use a Hypertext link before you've defined it. Just click OK to get past the pop-up box and find out what you missed. Before you can create the link, you've got to create a Bookmark in the text — so start there. For more about creating Hypertext links, see *InfoWorld WordPerfect 6 SECRETS*.

You Know You're in Trouble When . . .

Your screen flashes out and you hear a "bombing" sound

Anything truly weird like this scenario should be treated as a symptom of a computer virus. Contact your witch doctor and don't do anything yourself — you could make it worse. While the witch doctor is trying to salvage your data, ask about a routine backup and anti-virus checking plan that can help you practice safe PCing.

It was bound to happen: sooner or later you'd end up in one of these weird forests again. The symbols on the rocks get stranger every time. No one really knows where they came from. Some of the natives say it must be the gods. You're thinking maybe aliens.

Your hard disk crashes and you don't have a backup

Where else to preach about backups but in a chapter on files? Backup, backup, backup. Keep copies of important files. And keep copies of the copies of those important files. Someday, you may be very glad you did. And if that someday never comes, at least you'll know that you were ready for it.

Part II

Where Do
I Go Now?

Things could be worse. You could be in a place where it's really cold or something. Or maybe a place where there are a lot of boring conservations. You could be at a football game where your favorite team is losing. Or listening to your mother-in-law complain that you never get off the couch. Yeah, there must be some place worse than here . . . .

Chapter 5

Formatting Fiascoes

Paths through Peril

You're never too picky when you're trying to find shelter in the middle of a ferocious storm. Doesn't have to look good — doesn't even have to smell good. But in the light of day, appearance is more important. A little organization and order can make a big difference.

Too Many Tabs

Poison: Cursory interruptions

You're creating a simple memo. You include an introductory paragraph, two columns, and a concluding paragraph. But the to get data for the columns to line up, you have to press Tab, Tab, Tab, before the data. For each column. For every single line. That's just too many tabs.

Antidote: You can delete WordPerfect's default tabs (which are set at every .5 inch across the document) and add your own so that when you press Tab, the

This time, maybe you've gone a little too far.

cursor moves right to the place that you specify. Simply move the cursor to the place just in front of where you want to start the new tab settings, open the Layout menu, and choose Tab Set. Click Clear All (don't worry — we'll put them back), click the place on the ruler where you want the first tab, and then click the tab type (Left, Right, Center, or Decimal) that you want. After you add the second tab the same way, click on OK. When you return to the document, your tabs are set.

Note: For more about the ins, outs, and upside downs of tab settings, see *WordPerfect For Dummies* by Dan Gookin.

Broken Tabs

Poison: Tabs that don't work

You set the tabs the way that you were supposed to. You returned to the document and pressed the Tab key, expecting to see your data shoot across the screen. Nothing happened.

Antidote: Ask yourself the following questions:

▶ *Was the cursor positioned in the right place when you set the tab?* Put the cursor in front of the text that you want the new tab settings to affect.

▶ *Is Typeover mode on?* Look for Typeover in the bottom left corner of your screen.

▶ *Did you set the tabs properly?* Review the steps for setting tabs in *WordPerfect For Dummies.*

▶ *Did you click on the tab type before you clicked OK?* WordPerfect doesn't see the tab setting until you click on the tab type (Left, Right, Center, or Decimal). If you click OK without choosing a type, WordPerfect doesn't register the tab.

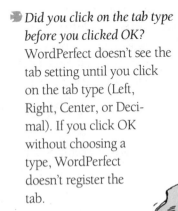

If Typeover mode is not in effect, try looking at Reveal Codes (press Alt-F3) to see whether the [Tab Set] code is in the correct general vicinity. If the tabs still aren't working properly, put the cursor where you want the tabs to begin and repeat the tab-selection process.

Copy-Cat Tabs

Poison: Text adopting old tabs

You're trying to finish up a report that you've been working on all day. After reading through the rough draft, you decide to go back into the middle and add a few paragraphs. When you start entering text, it is indented strangely.

Antidote: This problem could be related to several things:

- *Is there a style in effect in the area where you clicked the mouse?* If you positioned the cursor in an area where a style with a particular format — such as a hanging indent — is being used, the text you enter adoptd that format. Find out whether a style is in effect by pressing Alt-F8. If None is highlighted, no style is in effect.

- *Did you accidentally delete the code that returns the default tabs to normal?* Check and see by choosing Reveal Codes from the View menu.

- *Is Typeover mode in effect?* If so, you may have typed over and re-placed the codes that control the tab and indent settings. If your screen says Typeover in the bottom left corner, press Ins to return to Insert mode.

Most causes for inappropriate tab behaviors are missing or moved tab codes. The best tool you have for tab fixing is Reveal Codes, so if you work with tabs often, get friendly with Alt-F3.

Tabs Aren't for Tables?

Poison: Uncooperative tabs

When you enter text in your table, you press Tab to get from cell to cell. But that means that you can't use Tab the regular way — to align text in the way that you want it.

Antidote: WordPerfect gives you the option of using hard tabs in your tables so that you can align data as you want. Press Home and Tab to enter

Words of Wisdom:

Special Codes

Special codes let you change the format of a specific section of text when you don't want to make sweeping changes that affect the rest of your document. The codes include hard tabs, hard spaces, and hyphenation codes. Choose Special Codes from the Layout menu.

Note Types

With WordPerfect, you can enter a variety of additional notes to your basic document. You can include headers and footers, a watermark, footnotes, endnotes, and comments. All these extras are available in the Layout menu.

a left tab in a table; Home and Alt-F6 for a right tab; Home and Shift-F6 for a center tab; and Home and Ctrl-F6 for a decimal tab.

No-Turn-Off Margins

Poison: Temporary margins that aren't

You finished entering your list, pressed Enter a couple of times, and started typing the final paragraph of your paper. But your text is still indenting to the temporary margin that you selected for the list. Doesn't WordPerfect know that the subsequent text is supposed to be a paragraph?

Antidote: WordPerfect is still using the margin setting from the preceding section. Formatting codes remain in effect until you replace them with something else. If, for example, you specify a 2-inch indent for a list and then try to type a paragraph, the paragraph also will be indented 2 inches. In order to return the paragraph to normal style, position the cursor before the paragraph, open the Layout menu, and, in the Paragraph Margins section, change the Left Margin setting back to 0.

Down Under with Back Tab

Poison: No in-the-margin printing

You need all the space you can get on the document page, so you set up a back tab that enables you to print in the left margin. The Back Tab is like the Margin Release key on the old typewriter (in fact, it's *called* Margin Release in WordPerfect 5.1). Press Ctrl-Tab and WordPerfect lets you enter text in the margin area. But when you go to print the document, the characters that you entered in the margin are cut off.

Antidote: You must be using a laser printer. Laser printers have a built-in page margin of .25 inch all around the page. If you don't set your margins any lower than .25 (and don't use Back Tab or Margin Release), all your text should print.

How to Create Reusable Layouts

It's no secret that when you first start using WordPerfect, the number of available options swarm around you like killer bees. You desperately hope that you can avoid as many of them as possible.

But as your experience with WordPerfect grows, you begin to see a certain repetitiveness in your documents. You always enter your greeting the same way; you always use the same font and headline in the newsletter; you always write press releases in the same format.

Why choose those same options over and over again when you can create your own template file to store the documents that you use often? The next time that you're working on the press release, use the File menu's Save As command to make another copy of the document. Name the file something like PRESSREL.TPL. When you later go to write a press release, you can open PRESSREL.TPL and the basic format and font choices are already in there; all you have to do is replace the old text with the new (and remember to use Save As to name the file under a different name so that you don't replace the template).

WordPerfect 6 comes with four predesigned templates into which you can plug your own data: FAX.TEM, a fax cover sheet; LETTER.TEM, a template for a business letter; MEMO.TEM, a typical memo; and NEWSLTR.TEM, a template for a two-column newsletter.

What to Tell the Witch Doctor about Your Problem

Be ready to tell the witch doctor everything you know about your computer's symptoms as best you can (and with as little embellishment as possible):

- What problem occurred and/or what apparently died
- Any deathbed error messages that your computer gasped before expiring
- When it last worked correctly (if ever)
- Any changes in the environment (office remodeling)
- The last thing you did before the trouble hit
- Who touched it last
- What's been done to the machine recently (new software, hardware, network connection)
- First time, sporadic, or recurring problem
- What you've tried
- What you think the problem may be
- Anything else you can think of

Don't be offended if the witch doctor asks you to go back through some steps that you've already tried. He's probably checking for clues so small and technical that you didn't notice them.

Scrunched Headers

Poison: Too much text in too little space

You thought it would be cool to add a header to your document so that the managers would know that (1) you have mastered WordPerfect, and (2) you know what day it is. But when you print the document, the text is pushed right up against the header line.

Antidote: WordPerfect automatically inserts some space after the header and before the footer in your document. If you've changed the top or bottom margins, however, or if you have a multiline header or footer, the two different text items may be battling for page space. After you enter the header text, press Enter to add a blank line (if you're adding a footer, press Enter *before* the text). This trick should help spread things out a bit.

Heads and Feet in the Wrong Place

Poison: Misplaced appendages

You added a header and footer to your document, but they don't appear on the printout until page 3. You want them on all document pages.

Antidote: This situation can be caused by a couple of things:

Spaced Out?
Don't use up too much of your page margins. White space on the page is almost as important as the words; it gives readers' eyes a break.

➦ *Did you select All Pages in the Header or Footer dialog box?* You can find out by opening the Layout menu, choosing Header/Footer/ Watermark, clicking on the header or footer name you created (A or B), and seeing which of the three options — All Pages, Even Pages, or Odd Pages — is selected.

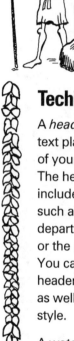

▶ *Did you create the header or footer when the cursor was positioned at the beginning of page 1?* If not, your problem is a case of a misplaced code. Go to the beginning of page 3 and turn on Reveal Codes (by pressing Alt-F3) to see whether that culprit is hiding there. If so, delete the code and re-create the header after you press Home, Home, up-arrow key to move to the beginning of the document.

No Need to Justify Yourself

Poison: Full-figure footers

You finished writing your document, added a footer, and took a look at your creation in Page Mode. You press PgDn to see how the footer looks. Nope, it's not right. It doesn't stretch all the way to the right margin.

Antidote: Even though documents look fine when they are left-justified, footers often look strange if they don't stretch all the way across the page. You can full-justify the footer by opening the Layout menu, choosing Header/Footer/Watermark, selecting the Footer name and Edit, and positioning the

Techie Term

A *header* is a line of text placed in the top of your document. The header can include information such as your name, department, the date, or the page number. You can control header text alignment as well as font and style.

A *watermark* is an item — such as a logo or graphic image — that is printed in the background of a printed page. The document text is printed over the watermark.

cursor at the beginning of the footer. Then open the Layout menu, choose Justification, and select Full.

Page Number Panics

Poison: Need nontraditional numbers

You put the cursor where you wanted it in the document and pressed Ctrl-P. A 1 appeared on-screen. But that's not what you need. You want to see a Roman numeral I.

Antidote: Open the Layout menu, choose Page, and select Page Numbering. Choose Page Number and then Numbering Method. Select the type of page number that you want from the drop-down list box.

Techie Term

The *justification* of text refers to the way the text is positioned in a column. Text that is left-justified aligns only along the left margin; right-justified text aligns only on the right. Full-justified text aligns along both margins. Centered text is centered between the margins.

Missing Page Mode

Poison: Invisible Page Mode

You've been working — somewhat smoothly — in Text Mode. So far, so good. You figured out how to indent, change margins, select a font, and add a footer. Now you want to take a look at what you've done.

But when you open the View menu and choose Page Mode you see

```
File not found
```

Before you go out on a ledge, check out what dangers lie above and below.

Antidote: At first glance, it may seem that something in Page Mode is missing. But when you try Graphics Mode, and Print Preview, you get the same message.

This error is caused by a missing file. Look for this file in your WPC60DOS directory:

```
BMF08X16.WFW
```

Words of Wisdom:

Page Numbering Perks

With WordPerfect 6.0, you can change the page numbering scheme to one of five settings: Arabic numerals (the usual 1, 2, 3), lowercase Roman (i, ii, iii), uppercase Roman (I, II, III), and upper- or lowercase letters (A, B, C or a, b, c). You also can add text to your page numbers to produce chapter and volume numbers as well.

Desktop Publishing

Desktop publishing allows you to create a finished publication — complete with graphics and special text effects — right on your PC. Although WordPerfect is technically a word-processing program, it includes a number of desktop publishing features, which make it a good choice for producing documents such as brochures, booklets, manuals, and newsletters.

The display drivers are kept in the
WP60 directory, but the additional files
are in WPC60DOS. If you are missing
this file — or you blew away your
WPC60DOS directory — send an
offering the witch doctor's way.

Off-Center Centering

Poison: Noncentering text

You try to add a few headings to spruce
up your report and make the section
breaks clearer. You type a heading, put
it in the right font, and press Shift-F6
to center it. How come that heading
looks so far off to the right?

Techie Term

Line spacing refers to
the amount of space
between lines of text.
Paragraph spacing
refers to the amount
of space between
paragraphs.

Antidote: Some formatting codes affect how truly your text is centere
you've selected a different Paragraph Margin, for example, centering will
push your text farther to the right. To make sure that your text is centered
accurately, remove any unnecessary codes before you press Shift-F6.

Multiple Alignments

Poison: Wanting text both ways

You tried fixing the header so that the title was left-justified and the page
number was right-justified. WordPerfect wouldn't oblige.

Antidote: One of the biggest advances of WordPerfect is also one of its
biggest problems: often there is more than one way to do the same thing.
For example, when you want to center text, you can use Layout Justification Center or Layout Alignment Center.

When you want to use more than one alignment, use the Alignment option in the Layout menu. In this case, type the document title and then press Alt-F6 (or select Layout Alignment Flush Right). The cursor moves to the right margin and you can enter the right-justified text.

Spacey Text

Poison: Full-justified problems

You've created a full-justified document — but in some places, the amount of space between

Before you go out on a limb, make sure that it can support you.

characters and words is huge, and in other places, the letters are pushed together.

Antidote: When you choose Full text justification, WordPerfect does what it must to make the text line up along both margins. To produce this effect, WordPerfect compresses and expands the space between the characters and words in your document. If WordPerfect is going overboard, you can control the percentage of expansion or compression allowed by selecting Layout Other, choosing Printer Functions, and changing the percentages in Word Spacing Justification Limits.

Where's the Line Spacing?

Poison: Unresponsive space settings

You changed one section in your document so that it would have more space between text lines. But you can't see any obvious difference after you made the change.

Antidote: You can make sure that WordPerfect recorded your change by moving the cursor to the point where the setting was selected and choosing Reveal Codes (Alt-F3). If the code is there, take a look at the document in Page Mode. The individual line spacing changes may not show up on your screen in text mode.

Cramped Paragraphs

Poison: Too-full page

You are almost finished with your document when you page back through to take a look at what you've done. You display Page Mode and notice that your document is a series of huge text blocks. The thought of reading back through it one more time makes your eyes water.

This is one of those times when you take an unintentional leap of faith . . . .

Antidote: A little space can do a lot to enliven a boring or intimidating paragraph. If you're working with large blocks of text, add some space between paragraphs to give readers' eyes a break. To do this task, open the Layout menu and choose Margins and Paragraph Spacing. The default value is one line. Increase this value to add to the white space between paragraphs that fall after the code in your document.

Column Clutter

Poison: Columns disrupt things

You thought that using the column feature would give a neat look to the corporate newsletter that you're trying to create, but instead, the columns just appear to jumble the text and make things hard to read.

Antidote: As a general rule, you will be happier with your document if you plan it out before you create it on-screen. Turning a single-column document into a multicolumn document on the spur of the moment may cause results that you didn't want or expect. Before you turn a single-column document into a multicolumn one, consider these tips:

- Keep heads short.
- Use a font, style, and alignment that looks good in columns.
- Consider where your art will go.
- Remember to leave enough space between columns.
- Vary the layout so that you don't have the same columns running the entire length of the document.
- Avoid overusing hyphenation because many hyphenated words in one column will distract the reader.

Whether you are desktop publishing a newsletter or doing a corporate report that requires multiple columns, taking a few minutes up front to plan out where you want important document elements to go can save you from endless cutting and pasting later.

Column Removal

Poison: Get 'em outta here

Those columns look *awful*! What can you do?

Antidote: Display the codes in your document by choosing Reveal Codes (press Ctrl-F3). Now move the cursor to the column code, [Col Def], and press Del. There. All gone.

Column Prolongus

Poison: Columns that go on forever

You finally set up columns for page 3 and they look pretty good. But then you notice that that page 4 has three columns, too. And so has page 5, and page 6. . . .

Antidote: Move the cursor to the point where you want the columns to stop. Open the columns drop-down list in the Ribbon (at the top of your screen). Click the down arrow and then choose 1 Col (if that's what you want). The document readjusts itself from that point on.

Out-of-Alignment Columns

Poison: Columns that won't line up

You included columns in your document to show information in the best possible way. You made a few changes to the font and style so that the columns would really look nice. But when you view the document in Page Mode, the columns look out of alignment.

Antidote: After you make font changes in columns, it's best to have WordPerfect realign things — just to make sure that everything's all right. Open the Layout menu and use Other Advance to have WordPerfect realign the columns (either up or down from the cursor) as you specify.

No Text at the Table

Poison: No-text table

You opened the Layout menu, chose Table, and then selected Create. When the pop-up box appeared, you entered the number of desired rows and columns. Then the table appears, and you try to type the column names. Every time you press a letter, a dialog box appears. You can't enter anything. What good is this table feature if you can't type text?

Antidote: What you're looking at is the Table Editor, which you use to specify settings such as Column Width, Text attributes, and formatting characteristics. Click on (Close) in the bottom right corner of the screen and you are returned to your WordPerfect document with the table intact. Now you can enter your data.

Techie Term

A *cell*, in table talk, is the intersection of a column and a row. It's the place where you enter that important piece of data or label.

The Table That Wouldn't Die

Poison: No-go table

You don't like the way the table is working out. You decide to delete it. So you highlight everything and press Del. Hey — wait a minute. The blan table is still sitting there.

Antidote: In order to get rid of a table, you must highlight all of it — cc and all — before you press Del. So take a look at Reveal Codes by press Alt-F3. The culprit that makes your table continue to hang out when yo are trying to get rid of it is the [Tbl Def] code (for table definition). It appears right before the first table line.

Gridlock!

Poison: Grids that won't leave

The data looks fine, now that you've entered it, but you don't like the way this box looks. Can you delete the grid without deleting the data?

Antidote: Remember that [Tbl Def] code you can see in Reveal Codes? Move the cursor to that code and delete it. Your text will remain, safe and sound.

You Know You're Really in Trouble When . . .

You've made major changes to your document format and don't like the look when you're through

It's always a good idea to make a safety copy (in addition to your most recent backup) before you do any major format revisions on an important — or lengthy — document. Just stick a disk in drive A and , as you go through the reformat process, copy the current document to disk. For example, you may make a copy of the original before changes (DOC1.DOC), after you create columns (DOC2.DOC), after you add tables (DOC3.DOC), and after you finalize margins, tabs, indents, page breaks, and font choices (DOC4.DOC). That way, if you decide that you don't like any of the result, you can return to a previous version of the document. For large documents, saving takes only a minute, but re-creating can take hours.

You highlighted the data in the table and tried to cut and paste it to a new location but WordPerfect put all the data in one cell.

Use Table Edit mode. Click inside the table and press Alt-F11 (or open the Layout menu and choose Table, Edit). Highlight the cells that you want to move and choose Move/Copy from the Table Editor. Select Block; move the cursor to the place where you want the data to go and press Enter.

Note: Any data that you paste in a new location will overwrite data already there. If you need to add rows or columns before you move the data, use the Table Edit Ins command.

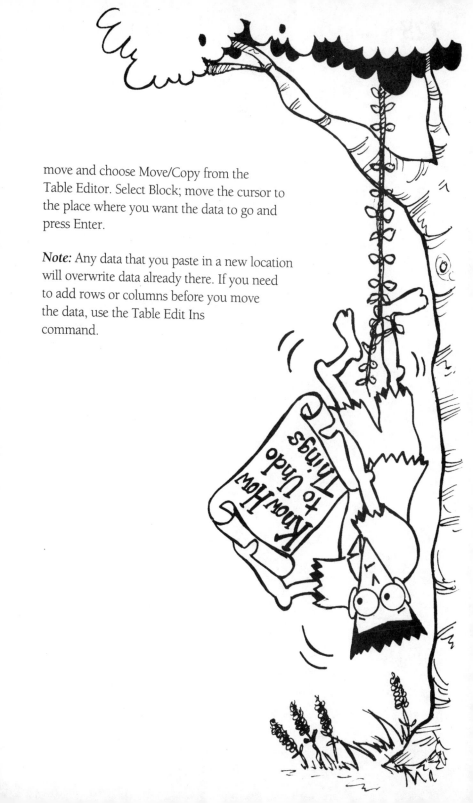

Chapter 6 — Unfriendly Fonts

Paths through Peril

It seems as if mere *words* won't do anymore — now you have to worry about the "look" of your prose almost as much as its content. This chapter puts you in command of fonts that let your text speak for itself: "*I'm happy!*" "I'M SAD." "I want your money."

"I Got No Fonts on Me . . ."

Poison: Your printer can't do the "fonts" thing — it dates back to a day when words were words (by golly!) and fonts came on daisy wheels.

Antidote: Almost any printer will give you *some* font choice (and if any program can get the most out of a printer, it's WordPerfect). But your printer *will* limit your choices if it can't print graphics because your most flexible font options are graphics fonts (this is where daisy-wheel printers come up short compared to laser printers). As long as you have a laser, ink-jet, or relatively youthful dot-matrix printer, you should have access to more than just the printer's built-in fonts. Notice that I said "should," not "will" — nothing in this life is guaranteed, and fonts are no exception.

Font Installation Fracas

Poison: You purchase a font package and install it just like the box says, but WordPerfect doesn't seem to notice your new acquisitions.

Antidote: This installation business is a two-step process, and you completed step one only. Step two involves introducing your new, visually stunning fonts to WordPerfect (and seeing that they hit it off well).

Beware
of
Falls

Because WordPerfect is an old-fashioned sort of software, it comes with a special electronic parlor for just such romantic interludes: the Font Installer. Here's how to begin the happy courtship between font and program, word and processor, thought and graphical representation (sniff, sniff — it's so beautiful, I think I'm going to cry).

Note: Before beginning this process, you need to know the name of the directory that contains your new font files. Look back through the font installation documentation if you aren't sure. If you still can't figure it out, consult your witch doctor for help.

1. **Select Font, Font, Setup from the menus (or press Ctrl-F8 and then Shift-F1).** Now you're in the Font Setup dialog box.

2. **Press 9 to install the fonts.** This step starts WordPerfect's Font Installer program.

3. **Choose the kind of font you're installing.** This information should be listed on the font box or in the documentation.

4. **WordPerfect displays a list of fonts available for installation.** If WordPerfect asks what directory your fonts are in, it means that the program looked in its default font directory and didn't find anything to install. Enter the name of the font directory in place of WordPerfect's default directory entry and then click on OK (or press Enter). If the font listing *still* doesn't appear, something just isn't working. Contact your witch doctor (or font manufacturer) for assistance.

5. **All fonts available for installation are marked with an asterisk (*).** If you want to exclude a font, use the arrow keys to highlight it and then press Enter to remove the asterisk. If you accidentally remove the asterisk from a font you want to install, just highlight it and press Enter again.

6. **After marking the fonts you want to install, press 2 to start the installation.** WordPerfect works through each font, displaying a dialog box that tells you how it's doing. After the installation is complete, another dialog box appears, offering to let you escape the installation program. Unless you're installing more fonts, press Enter to exit the program. If you have more fonts to install, tab to the Continue button

and press Enter. WordPerfect then takes you back to the Select Font
Type dialog box, where you can continue installing fonts to your
heart's content.

Your new fonts are now available in WordPerfect, provided that your
printer can support them (WordPerfect will worry about that for you). If
your printer can't support a font that you installed, WordPerfect simply
won't let you apply that font to your text.

Font Installer in the Dark

Poison: When you try to use the WordPerfect Font Installer to install your
new fonts, it doesn't list your fonts in the Available Fonts dialog box. You
entered the correct path and the files are in the right place, so what's going
on?

Antidote: For one reason or another, WordPerfect doesn't think that the
files you specified are *real* font files. You need to check several things:

> *Are you installing the fonts as the right kind of font?* WordPerfect
> supports several different font standards, and each is very different.
> Look at the documentation that came with the fonts. Do you see
> designations such as Type 1, TrueType, Speedo, or Intellifont? In the
> Font Installer, select the appropriate installation option and try again.

> *Is the Font Installer looking in the right directory?* Of course, you
> already should have checked out this possibility, but I just thought I'd
> ask again. It never hurts to look one more time.

> *Try reinstalling the fonts.* Perhaps something just went wrong the first
> time.

> *If the installer still doesn't see the fonts, get your witch doctor.* Some-
> thing is making WordPerfect think that your fonts aren't compatible
> with any of the WordPerfect standards. You've done everything you
> can; leave this one to the expert.

Sometimes matters just seem
to get worse and worse.
Forget appearances —
this is survival.

How to Get the Fonts You So Richly Deserve

So you only have a few fonts in WordPerfect, despite the fact that your super-deluxe laser printer is capable of using graphics fonts. Hmmm. There's only one thing to do:

Go get more fonts!

WordPerfect 6 directly supports all the major font standards (Type 1, TrueType, Bitstream Speedo, and printer-specific soft fonts). In other words, WordPerfect doesn't need any other program to help it work with a particular kind of font. Not all software is this bright — some packages need an electronic sidekick just to keep the fonts in line.

Depending on the quality and manufacturer, fonts range in price from free to over $100 each. Many companies (such as Bitstream and Microsoft) sell font packs containing several related fonts, and numerous shareware software companies list TrueType fonts in their catalogs.

The advantage of shareware fonts is that you can build your font collection at a reasonable cost. And you can try them before you buy. Consult your witch doctor for specific recommendations on good-for-you fonts.

Words of Wisdom: The Lingo of Fontifornia

This whole font thing is about being cool. Not just cool, but *way cool*. And the key to way cool WordPerfect fonts is a type of fonts called *graphics fonts*.

Graphics fonts are *scalable* (you can print them at any size you like); work with many different printers (important for you document-swappers); and take just a little disk space. It doesn't get much better than this.

The standards are

- *Type 1* fonts follow Adobe's standard for font scaling (originally developed for PostScript printing).

- *TrueType* fonts came from Apple and Microsoft. The scaling technology used by these is now directly supported in WordPerfect 6.0.

- *Speedo* fonts are from Bitstream. They have a reputation as fast screen and printing fonts.

- *Intellifont* is Agfa's standard. Hewlett-Packard printers often ship with Intellifont screen fonts to match the printer's built-in font set.

Of Course There Are Fonts There!

Poison: When you run through the Font, Font, Setup, Select Graphics Fonts menu gauntlet, the Select Graphics Fonts option is grayed-out. WordPerfect won't let you select the option, despite the fact that you paid out the wazoo for oodles of graphics fonts and spent the better part of yesterday installing them.

Antidote: Before I begin, let me remind you that flying books are a serious safety issue, ranking on the office hazard list right up there with spilled white-out.

With that thought in mind, select File, Setup, Location of files (or press Shift-F1, 5) and make sure that the setting for WP.DRS file and *.WFW files is correct. If not, change it to point to the subdirectory where your WP.DRS file is cowering.

If the directory setting is already correct — or if you just used WordPerfect's defaults for everything, in which case there's no reason for the setting to be incorrect — you may have lost your .DRS file (you know, the one that tracks all your graphics fonts). You need to reinstall it from your original WordPerfect distribution disks (see "WP.DRS file not found" in the "Reading Smoke Signals" section at the end of this chapter for more information). Then use the Font Installer to reload all those graphics fonts. Really, I'm sorry — please don't throw this book.

Back Up Your WP.DRS File

Always have a backup of your WP.DRS file. Copy the file onto a floppy disk or even to another hard disk directory. You'll find the file in your C:\WPC60DOS directory (or elsewhere if you customized your WordPerfect directories).

It Picked an Ug-lee Font

Poison: WordPerfect always uses the same font when you create a document, and (eek!) the one it uses offends your delicate visual sensitivities.

Antidote: It's easy to resolve this problem and soothe your poor sensitivities. The key is in the Font Setup dialog box:

1. **Select Font, Font, Setup from the menu (or press Ctrl-F8, Shift-F1).** The Font Setup dialog box appears.

2. **Press 1. Select Initial Font.**

3. **Press 1 again to choose the font.** Press Enter or click on the font of your dreams. If you want to change the font size as well, press 2 and select a size (after you choose the

font). If WordPerfect only gives you one choice for font size, you selected a fixed-size font.

4. **Tell WordPerfect whether you want to use the new font in the current document only or in all future documents.** Granted, this decision has far-reaching implications, but I think that you can make it on your own. If you're unsure for more than five minutes, change the font just in the current document and see how you like "the new you." You can always change the font to something else later.

5. **Click on Exit or press F10 to save your changes.**

Note: Each printer driver has its own default font setting. The change you just made affects *only* the current printer driver. If you regularly change between two printers, you need to change to the other driver and select a new default font *there* as well.

When Fido-Font Won't Stay Put

Poison: You changed the font, but it won't stay changed. Every now and then, it reverts back to the default setting on its own.

Antidote: Every time you select a new font, WordPerfect inserts one of those little hidden codes into your document. You're probably typing

Words of Wisdom: Choosing Fonts for Easy Document Sharing

If you swap documents among a group of people, get together and establish a standard set of fonts to use on shared documents. I recommend that you use graphics fonts so that you won't be dependent on a certain kind of printer. Make sure that all members of the group have the selected fonts available on their computers and that all the printers can handle all the fonts. By planning ahead, you'll save hours of time later (particularly if there's a crunch on and you need that document *now*). Get your witch doctor's advice if you don't know how to get the fonts you need or want some help deciding which fonts to use.

outside of the codes, so WordPerfect thinks that you want the text formatted with the default settings. (I could say that the program is only doing what it's supposed to do, but I always find it annoying when people say that to me.)

To solve the mystery, turn on Reveal Codes (select View, Reveal Codes or press Alt-F3). Look for the font codes surrounding your text. You should see (apart from a morass of curiously punctuated computer codes) something that looks like the following text. (This example assumes that your default font is Courier.)

```
Normal Courier text — as normal as computer text ever is
— appears here. [+Font:Antique Olive] This text will
print in Antique Olive. [-Font:Courier] Now we're back to
Courier, in all its inherent beauty (yeah, and pigs fly,
too).
```

As long as your text falls between the code that turns on Antique Olive (the code with the plus sign (+) in it) and the code returning Courier to power (the -Font code), it should print in Antique Olive. If your codes are a mishmash, ask your witch doctor to help you figure out what's going on.

Fonts That Don't Travel Well

Poison: Although the document was a work of art on *your* printer, it looks like a ransom note when your coworker prints it.

Antidote: Compare the printers at each workstation (I think that you'll solve this problem on your own). It's likely that the two of you don't have the same printer. Even worse, you may have completely different types of printers — you have a laser, for example, and your colleague has a dot matrix. If that's the case, the printers don't, by nature, have any fonts in common. If you used *internal* (printer-specific) fonts in your document, WordPerfect must substitute whatever fonts are available on your coworker's system in order to print the document. This substitution can lead to *messafontitis*, a malady that causes affected documents to get that really weird ransom-note look.

Avoid this horrible disease by using graphics fonts on documents you're going to share with other people. If you and your coworkers have some fonts in common and graphics-capable printers, the document will look nearly the same (except for differences in printer resolution) no matter who prints it.

Dull Bolds and Lazy Italics

Poison: The font codes in your document are correct, but some of your fonts won't print in italics, bold, or a combination of the two.

Antidote: I'll bet that you're using a built-in printer font. Find out by clicking on one of

the appropriately formatted words and pressing Ctrl-F8 (or selecting Font, Font from the menu) to display the Font dialog box.

At the top left of the dialog box, WordPerfect displays the current font type: built-in or graphics. If it says graphics, you have an interesting problem. WordPerfect works very hard to create italic, bold, and bold-italic versions of graphics fonts, regardless of what you installed. Better ask the witch doctor to have a look at your system — it sounds a little weird.

Techie Term

Scaling a font doesn't mean getting out your ropes and pitons for a nice, refreshing climb. If your printer can scale fonts, it can change their size without any assistance from WordPerfect. Low-end printers can't do the job. They need WordPerfect to change the font's size and then spoon-feed them with the information.

On the other hand, if the font type entry says that you're using built-in fonts, I can *explain* what's going on, even if I can't fix it for you (oops, I let that one slip a little early).

A given printer may have Courier as a built-in font. Not only does it have Courier Upright (normal), it also has Courier Italic, Courier Bold, and Courier Bold Italic. Not all printers are alike: Some merely double-print a character to simulate boldface type or slant it forward to make pretend italics. Some can't even go that far and just substitute something simple, like underlines, when pressed for a look they can't produce.

The ultimate moral of the story (once again) is to try graphics fonts when your printer doesn't quite do what you want. In fact, it's a good idea to get in the habit of using graphics fonts in general because they transfer more accurately — an important consideration if the document ever finds a new home or if you get a new printer.

Limited Size Offer, Call Now!

Poison: Some fonts give you a wide variety of sizes, but others give you only one and make you feel guilty about asking for more.

Antidote: You're back to the graphics font versus built-in font battle-ground. Many printers can't scale fonts on their own. When you select a built-in font with one of these printers, you have one size choice. If you want a different size, you must choose a different font.

Graphics fonts, however, can be sized by WordPerfect to suit your mood, regardless of your printer's capabilities. Once again, graphics fonts triumph for versatility, power, and raw willingness to serve. (And the crowd goes wild. . . .)

Hijacking Windows Fonts

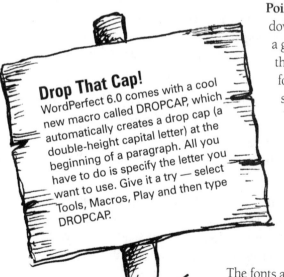

Drop That Cap!
WordPerfect 6.0 comes with a cool new macro called DROPCAP, which automatically creates a drop cap (a double-height capital letter) at the beginning of a paragraph. All you have to do is specify the letter you want to use. Give it a try — select Tools, Macros, Play and then type DROPCAP.

Poison: As a covert Windows user, you've amassed a group of TrueType fonts that you're particularly fond of. But they don't show up in WordPerfect. What a cruel hoax — is this some kind of Microsoft trick?

Antidote: Because we're dealing with TrueType fonts, this case is nearly solved.

The fonts are already installed on your computer (otherwise, they wouldn't work with Windows). All you have to do is run WordPerfect's Font Installer and add them to the list.

Follow the instructions in the "Font Installation Fracas" section earlier in this chapter and specify C:\WINDOWS\SYSTEM (or C:\WIN\SYSTEM, depending on your installation) as the TrueType directory. Those fonts never had a chance with you around. Good work, gumshoe.

The Disappearing Paragraph

Poison: Although you see text on-screen, it doesn't appear on your printout. You've tried every font (even the grody-looking ones you never use), but the text still won't come out on the page. Is it *afraid* to print? What's it doing, *hiding* somewhere?

Antidote: Funny you should put it that way. That's exactly what your text is doing.

WordPerfect 6.0 includes the capability to hide text in a document. A new menu option under Font, Hidden Text (or Alt-F5, 7 for you keyboard fans out there) enables you to format text as "hidden" and tell WordPerfect whether you want to display hidden text. Of course, with any new feature, some teensy-weensy little problems and misunderstandings are bound to crop up:

- *To create hidden text, block the text you want to hide and then open the Hidden Text dialog box by selecting Font, Hidden Text (or Alt-F5, 7). Press 1 and then Enter.* WordPerfect inserts hidden text codes around the blocked text, and you never have to worry about that text printing out again.

- *To undo the process, make sure that WordPerfect is displaying hidden text.* Get into the Hidden Text dialog box and look for an X next to the option named Show All Hidden Text. Block the hidden text that you want to rescue and then follow the steps above. WordPerfect then turns the hidden mode off for the blocked text.

Warning: If WordPerfect isn't set to display hidden text, don't turn on Reveal Codes (Alt-F3) and try to manually unhide any hidden text. When WordPerfect isn't displaying hidden text, the text *itself* becomes part of the hidden code. Deleting the code *also deletes the text*. If you accidentally delete the code and text, just use undelete to bring it back (select Edit, Undelete, Restore or press Esc). Undelete does a fine job (I know; I learned the hard way).

Quick Wraps and Short Lines

Poison: You hacked around with fonts and sizes for a while. Now you're in text mode and you notice that WordPerfect will only let you type a few words on a line. Funny, it doesn't work that way farther up in the document. . . .

Antidote: During your round of formatting, you probably chose a larger-than-normal font size. Try switching over to Graphics mode (select View, Graphics from the menu or press Ctrl-F3, 3 on the keyboard). Is your text really big? Block it and reduce the size (choose a smaller point size from the ribbon or through the Font dialog box) to resolve the problem.

If font size isn't the problem, you may have accidentally changed your line width. See Chapter 5 for help with indents and other sundry matters.

What I See Isn't What I Get

Poison: The fonts don't print exactly like they look on-screen.

Antidote: WordPerfect 6.0 isn't a perfectly true WYSIWYG (What You See Is What You Get) program. It's pretty close but not totally there. But then, who really is?

If you're using a built-in printer font, WordPerfect has to wing it to create an appropriate, matching screen font to use in Graphics mode (View, Graphics). For "normal" fonts — like Times and Helvetica — WordPerfect does pretty well, thanks to its Dutch and Swiss fonts. For more esoteric printer fonts, like Coronet or Double-height Courier, WordPerfect can't quite pull off the stunt, so you have a WYSIAWYG (What You See Is *Almost* What You Get) display. Such is the way of these things.

Remember that the Print Preview mode gives you a *good idea* of how your finished page will look, not a precise proof of your work. Use it to save paper and check for gross formatting problems. Until technology moves further ahead, though, you'll still have to go through some trees while polishing the final draft.

Reading Smoke Signals

Fonts were installed or deleted from the .DRS file. . . . Do you want to update the .DRS file?

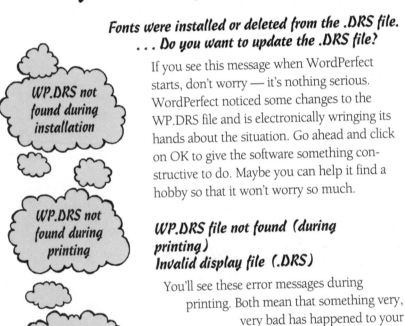

WP.DRS not found during installation

WP.DRS not found during printing

DRS files deleted

If you see this message when WordPerfect starts, don't worry — it's nothing serious. WordPerfect noticed some changes to the WP.DRS file and is electronically wringing its hands about the situation. Go ahead and click on OK to give the software something constructive to do. Maybe you can help it find a hobby so that it won't worry so much.

WP.DRS file not found (during printing) Invalid display file (.DRS)

You'll see these error messages during printing. Both mean that something very, very bad has happened to your WP.DRS file, which holds information on the graphics fonts you've installed. WordPerfect can't find the file, or the file is trashed — either way, you need to reinstall the file. Run the installation program and select option 4 (install printer drivers) and select 4 again. Replace the drivers for the printers you selected. WordPerfect creates a new .DRS file to replace the old one, which is now long gone to that disk drive in the sky.

WP.DRS file not found (during font installation)
File is locked
Invalid file type

These little ditties pop up in the WordPerfect Font Installer. They're all signs that your WP.DRS file is either missing (and presumed dead) or having an electronic bad hair day. It's time to get out those installation disks and reinstall the .DRS file. See the preceding section for instructions.

You Know You're Really in Trouble When . . .

You haven't saved your new file and get Divide Overflow (followed by machine lockup) during Print Preview

Divide Overflow is one of those marvelous messages that basically mean "something went wrong." If you get such messages every few months, they are probably anomalies (you're supposed to just live with them). If they come daily, you have a problem that some good witch doctor can resolve

for you. Concerning your document, the moral of the story is this: Always save your work first and *then* play with printing, previews, and other potential program pitfalls.

None of your 197 graphics fonts show up in the font list

Sounds like WordPerfect recently lost contact with your WP.DRS file. Cry now — get it out of your system — and then begin putting the fontographic pieces back together. Reinstall the WP.DRS file and then use the WordPerfect Font Installer to reinstall all 197 fonts. Of course, you also can just replace the WP.DRS file from your backup, provided you have one.

You get confused when thinking about Ctrl-F8 and Shift-F8

Ctrl-F8 (Font, Font, Font) puts a font code in the document at the point where the cursor is (or around a block of text). Shift-F8 sets the font for the entire document, regardless of cursor position, without including a code within the document. The latter is a much safer option for someone who wants to set a particular font for the entire document and who may be confused by codes.

Chapter 7

Graphics Gremlins and Sound Snafus

Paths through Peril

You can operate in survival mode only for so long before something inside whispers, "Lighten up — have some fun." You may want to spruce up your shelter or make a little island music, just to let off some steam.

Immovable Graphics

Poison: A mouse-ignoring graphics box

OK, you added a graphics box and even put a picture in it. But you want to move the box to another point in your document. You click on the box and nothing happens.

Antidote: In Text mode, the graphics boxes are used only to mark the place where art will be inserted. You can't click on the graphics box to move or resize it when you're in Text mode. You can, however, click the graphics box in Graphics or Page mode. Doing so causes the handles of the box to function and your pointer to change to either a four-headed arrow or a double arrow. You now can make changes to the graphics box.

Invisible Art

Poison: Blank graphics box

You just received the finished document from the marketing department. You've been waiting for it all day. But when you open the document and take a look at it in Graphics mode, the art is not in the graphics boxes where it should be.

Antidote: It's possible that the document was set up so that the art was stored on disk rather than embedded in the document. First, double-click the box and see what the Edit Graphics Box screen can tell you.

- *Are you sure that you're in Graphics mode?* (Sorry, had to ask.) To be sure, open the View menu and make sure that there's a check mark beside the Graphics Mode option.

- *Is there a name listed in Filename?* The name of the art file should be displayed there.

- *Is the Contents option set to Image or Image on Disk?* If Contents option is set to Image, the graphic should be embedded in your document file. If Image on Disk appears, WordPerfect expects to look on the disk for the necessary graphics file.

🔊 *Is the file saved in a format WordPerfect can recognize?* You can tell by the file's extension in the Filename: entry. See the nearby sign sidebars for lists of supported graphics file formats.

If the Contents option shows Image on Disk, search the disk for the file shown in the Filename option. If the file is not on the disk, contact the people who created the file: they forgot to send the art files you need.

If the Contents option says Image and there is an entry in the Filename option, something may be wrong with the art file. Try opening another graphics file — perhaps a file that takes up less memory — to see whether any graphics file will show up in the graphics box.

If you suspect that the problem is an incompatible graphics format, check with your witch doctor for some special magic to make those graphics files WordPerfect-friendly.

No-Show Graphics Mode

Poison: Unavailable graphics display

You've been working on your document for over an hour. You've got the text formatted just right. All the fonts for the heads and subheads have been chosen. Now you want to take a look at the thing in Graphics mode and see the result of your hard work before you print.

What? No Graphics mode — instead, a small box pops up to tell you "Sorry, no can do." You can click on Help to get a more empathetic explanation, but the bottom line is this: you can't see your document in any of the graphics modes — Graphics, Page, or even Print Preview — until you've freed up some RAM.

Antidote: Here are the questions you need to answer:

> *Do you have any other programs loaded in memory?* If so, exit WordPerfect, reboot, and don't load the other programs before you start WordPerfect.

WordPerfect 5.1 Likes These Graphics File Formats: CGM, DHP, DXF, EPS, GEM, HPGL, IMG, MNTG, MSP, PCX, PIC, PPIC, TIFF, and WPG.

> *Have you used a memory management program like MEMMAKER to optimize the available RAM?* (Better let the witch doctor help you with this one.)

> *Did you run WordPerfect from the Shell or from DOS?* Skipping the Shell can save you some memory.

> *Is adding RAM a possibility?* (Again, a question for the witch doctor.)

If you just plain don't have enough RAM and there's nothing you can do about it, don't despair — you can still use WordPerfect and print your documents. The program still works, but you haven't the means on-screen to check elements such as fonts, the format, headers and footers, and other graphic items. So you may have to print the document a few times to see whether you got it right. (But don't forget to ask for one or two megabytes for Christmas.)

Getting There Is Half the Fun

Poison: Problems moving through the document

You just switched over to Graphics mode for the first time. You added a couple of graphics boxes and pressed PgDn, hoping to page through the rest of the document. The cursor blinked. Nothing happened. Then — what was that? — after a few seconds, the screen moved.

Antidote: The display in Graphics mode can be extremely slow, especially if you're using some heavy-duty graphics. You can speed up the way you move through the document (and not be so dependent on the keyboard) by adding scroll bars.

By default, the scroll bars are not turned on when you start Graphics mode for the first time. Open the View menu and choose Vertical scroll bar (choose Horizontal if you need to skim left to right). Now you can use the scroll bar to view the different parts of your document.

WordPerfect 6.0 Digs These Graphics File Formats: BMP, CGM, EPS, GIF, HPGL, PCX, PIC, PICT, TIFF, WMF, and WPG.

No Scrolling Allowed

Poison: Hitting a wall

You added a graphics box at the end of
your document — because you intend to
later enter the text that comes before the
box — and WordPerfect won't let you see
the art. You can't scroll down past the last
character that you typed.

Antidote: When you add a graphic and
set it up to be attached to a paragraph,
WordPerfect looks for the paragraph to
which it's attached. The image is there,
but because the text isn't, you can't scroll
down through the document to see the
art. Press Enter until the graphic box is
visible. Now go back and enter your text.
(And remember to delete those extra
Enters later.)

Controlling Text Flow

Poison: Stopping runaway text

The document that you're producing will
include three head shots of corporate
leaders. You don't have a scanner, so
you'll be manually cutting and pasting in
the photos after the document is printed.
But you still need some way of marking
where the photos will go so that the text
doesn't run into the space.

Antidote: Add a user graphics box. You
want to specifically choose a user graph-

ics box because this box is the only kind that appears without a border. When you place the box, text flows automatically around it, thus preserving the blank space for the photo to come later.

Slippery Graphics

Poison: Wandering graphics box

The graphics box that you created won't stay with the text it is meant to accompany. When you move text around, the graphics box seems to float wherever it wants.

Antidote: Double-click on the graphics box and choose Attach To. To make the art stay with the paragraph preceding it, choose Paragraph.

Are-You-Still-Here? Graphics

Poison: Stuck-on-you graphics box

Now the graphics box stays with text and you don't want it to.

Antidote: If you want a piece of art to stay in a certain position on the page (for example, a logo that you've created for a particular document), double-click on the graphics box and choose Attach To in the Edit Graphics Box. Change the Paragraph setting to Fixed Page Position (available in WordPerfect 6.0 only).

Graphics Crowding

Poison: Need more personal space

After you add a graphics box, you see that the graphics box is too close to the document text. There's hardly any room at all.

Antidote: Double-click on the graphics box to display the Edit Graphics Box dialog box. Click on Edit Border/Fill and then choose Spacing. Uncheck the Automatic Spacing check box and enter your settings; then click on OK. This procedure should space out the text and your art image.

Note: Doing away with the graphics box border may help you gain more room in tight document layouts. Choosing a user box helps you bypass the border issue. You can also double-click on the existing graphics box, choose Edit Border/Fill, Select All, and None.

Art Bumping

Poison: Self-moving art

You don't want it to, but your art moves to the next page.

Antidote: If WordPerfect does not have enough room to place the graphics box on the current page, the box is moved to the next page. You can do several things to get around this problem:

- Make more room on the current page by changing the text font, style, or headings. (See *WordPerfect For Dummies* for the scoop on text changes.)

- Change the size of the graphics box. (Double-click on it and choose Edit Size; then enter your settings.)

- Consider reorganizing the document so that unnecessary text that is taking up room is moved to another page or deleted.

Make the graphics box a freestanding art element by double-clicking on it and choosing Attach To, Fixed Page Position. This option attaches the graphics box to the page in the position that you specify and won't allow it to be bumped to the next page.

It's so darned cold up here. And you're so tired. There's nothing quite like camping out at the higher elevations, especially when you have no choice.

How to Make Your Own Clip Art Library

Even artists reuse whatever works. If you have been working with a piece of clip art in WordPerfect by setting graphics box options and using the Edit Graphics Box dialog box, it's worth saving the final image. "Oh, but I didn't create it," you say. "I just modified it." If you plan to use the graphic again, save it out to disk under a unique name. It may come in handy later.

By default, WordPerfect saves all its graphics files in the WPGO/GRAPHICS directory, both before and after you modify them. You may want to create another directory — such as \GRAPHICS or \CLIPART — off your root directory so that you can store modified files in a place where your other applications can share them easily.

When you want to save your modified clip art, click on the Save As button in the Image Editor (where you make the modifications). In the Filename: box, specify the drive, directory, and filename for the modified clip art file. Then click on OK or press Enter.

If you use graphics in a variety of programs, you need a graphics file conversion utility, such as Hijaak or Graphics Workshop. These conversion/editing utilities allow you to change files from one format to another and are invaluable in changing the WPG WordPerfect graphics files into more widely acceptable formats like PCX or GIF.

What's the Best Way to Avoid Bad Witch Doctor Advice?

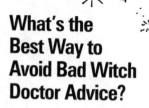

Some well-meaning witch-doctor-wanna-bes offer some pretty suspect advice at times. If you hear some of the following suggestions, you may want to get a second opinion before proceeding:

- *"You're just going to have to reformat your hard drive."* (This statement is rarely true.)

- *"Sorry, but your data's gone forever."* (Maybe you can use UNFORMAT or UNDELETE.)

- *"If you're sure you didn't create those files, go ahead and delete them."* (Those files may be network drivers — don't touch.)

- *"Oh, just turn your machine off and on a few times."* (Sometimes shutting the system down is your only option. But if you do it when you don't need to, you could lose your only chance of recovering your data.)

- *"Press Ctrl-Alt-Delete or Ctrl-Break — that'll do it."* (This is another one of those sometimes-it's-necessary pieces of advice. But you should try everything else first and reboot only as a last resort.)

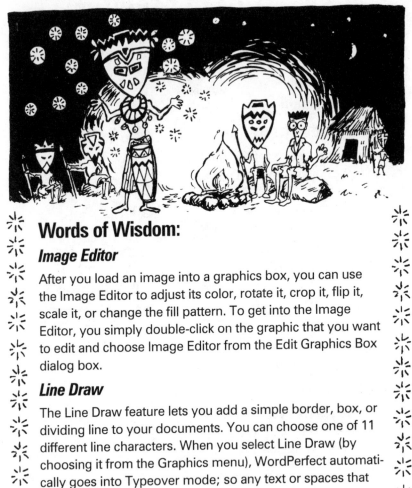

Words of Wisdom:

Image Editor

After you load an image into a graphics box, you can use the Image Editor to adjust its color, rotate it, crop it, flip it, scale it, or change the fill pattern. To get into the Image Editor, you simply double-click on the graphic that you want to edit and choose Image Editor from the Edit Graphics Box dialog box.

Line Draw

The Line Draw feature lets you add a simple border, box, or dividing line to your documents. You can choose one of 11 different line characters. When you select Line Draw (by choosing it from the Graphics menu), WordPerfect automatically goes into Typeover mode; so any text or spaces that you type over will be replaced with a line character.

Slowest Screen in the West

Poison: Snooze-em or lose-em screen updates

Graphics mode is agonizingly slow. Each time you make a text change, the screen wavers in a slowly descending update.

Antidote: Because Graphics mode is a graphical mode (no big surprise there), lots of things are going on when your screen is being updated. All the art has to be redrawn; your fonts have to be repositioned; and headers, footers, and other items have to be redone. For the best (that is, fastest) screen updates, use Text mode to do your basic text work — text entry, editing, and formatting. Then switch back to Graphics mode when you want to take a look at your art elements.

Big Mistake Art Editing

Poison: Wish you hadn't done that . . .

OK, so maybe you got a little carried away when changing the image in the Image Editor. You changed the brightness and contrast, rotated the art, flipped it horizontally, and changed the fill type. Boy, it looks awful.

Antidote: Luckily, there's an easy way out of the mess. Click on the Reset All button in the Image Editor's toolbar (fourth button from the left). WordPerfect returns the art to its pre-edited state.

Cutoff Art

Poison: Truncated image

You flipped the image (by using one of the Flip commands in the Image Editor), and after you click on Close to return to the Graphics mode screen, you see that that part of the image is cut off by the graphics box.

Techie Term

Clip art is already-done (prefab) art that you can use in your own publications. Some programs, like Word- Perfect, come with their own clip art and accept clip art from other manufacturers as well as art that you create yourself.

Antidote: You need to change the size of the graphics box to allow more room inside. Double-click on the image and choose Edit Size. You can have WordPerfect set the width and height by choosing Automatic or you can enter your own settings. For best results, enter a larger setting for either the width or height (or both); then click on OK.

Right-Wing Graphics

Poison: Graphics imbalance

Every graphics box that you've added so far in your document has put itself on the right side of the page. Looks a little one-sided, doesn't it? How can you tell WordPerfect to put an image on the other side of the page?

Antidote: This is a job for the Edit Graphics Box. Double-click on the image (or, if you haven't added it yet, select Graphics, Graphics Boxes, Create) and choose Edit Position. In Horizontal Position, choose Left. Click on OK (and OK) to return to the document. There you go — a more liberal piece of clip art.

Graphics (Under) Line?

Poison: Line or underline

You wanted to add a graphics line to separate two sections of text. But when you positioned the cursor, opened the Graphics menu, and selected the necessary commands to draw the line, WordPerfect put the graphics line under the line of text.

Antidote: When you add a graphics line, WordPerfect places it immediately after the cursor position. If your cursor is positioned on the first text line of a paragraph, when you add a graphics line, it is going to appear under the text. To put the line where it goes, make sure that you put the cursor on a blank line.

Pretty soon, you doze off and start dreaming. But you're so cold that the images passing through your mind take on a bizarre form. Seals, penguins, and polar bears — oh, my! Where's a Holiday Inn when you need one?

More Space for the Line, Please

Poison: Space-eating graphics lines

You added a graphics line on a blank line between two paragraphs and now everything is scrunched up together.

Antidote: When WordPerfect adds a graphics line, it replaces the blank line with the graphics line. This addition creates the appearance that your text paragraphs are pulled together even though the same amount of space still separates them (there's just a line in the middle). To get around this tight-space problem, be sure to give graphics lines plenty of room; add an extra line before and after graphics lines to help keep your document from looking too crowded.

Unwanted Art Elements

Poison: Too many boxes

You've added all this art to your document and now you're sorry you did. How do you get rid of all the graphics boxes and lines?

Antidote: If you're working in Graphics mode (which is, by far, the easiest for dealing with graphics), just point at the thing that you want to delete and press Del. WordPerfect will ask you if you're sure that you want to do something so destructive. After the appropriate amount of soul-searching, click on Yes.

Note: In a moment of passion (or desperation), you may on occasion delete something that you need to use later. To minimize such occurrences, before you make major changes to your document, save a copy of the file just in case you want it back at some later point.

What about Sound?

Poison: Not a peep

You have a sound board installed in your system. You've used it with other programs, so you know that it works. But when you try to use WordPerfect's Sound Clips feature, you get a message that sound isn't set up.

Antidote: If the message is still on-screen, click on OK or press Enter. The Sound Setup dialog box appears. If you've returned to the document, open the Tools menu and choose Sound Clip; then choose Sound Setup. Use the

options in the Sound Setup dialog box to tell WordPerfect what kind of sound board you have. When you return to the document, you should be able to use the Sound Clips feature.

Can You Hear Me?

Poison: Voice notes not recording

You have a new sound board in your computer and a burning desire to add speaking (or singing) notes to your document. You think that you've followed the directions correctly, but when you try to play the sound clip that you've created, you don't hear anything.

Antidote: The silence could be caused by several things:

- *Did you click on the Rec button (or press 1)?* The Rec button in the Record Sound Clip dialog box is what actually starts the recording process.

- *Is the microphone plugged in?* The microphone should plug into the jack on your sound board in the back of your computer.

- *Is your microphone turned on?* Some microphones have a small on/off switch on the side.

- *Is your sound board functioning properly?* Check the sound board's manual for instructions on how to find out. (Ordinarily, you'll find a self-test file that you can run to test the equipment.)

- *Is the volume turned up loud enough for you to hear?* You can set the volume in the Record Sound Clip dialog box. (Some sound boards also have manual volume controls on the back of the board.)

If you try all these things and can't uncover the problem, get ahold of the witch doctor. The problem could be with something really mysterious (and, as they say, lethal) like IRQs and memory addresses.

Reading Smoke Signals

They say music can tame the savage beast, but can it fix graphics problems? Probably not. (Doesn't work much for my children, either.) As you attempt to struggle through graphics and sound, you may see these smoke signals:

Not enough memory for graphics

WordPerfect needs more memory (like 520K) in order to run and use Graphics, Page, and Print Preview modes. All three are graphics modes and require more memory than simple Text mode. Try freeing up as much RAM as possible (and if you haven't run a memory optimizer, contact your witch doctor to help you do so) and then try WordPerfect again.

Sound Driver Status

If there's something going on with your sound board, WordPerfect will display the Sound Driver Status box along with a possible explanation of the problem. To find out how to resolve the trouble, check your sound board's documentation.

Sound setup required

Your system may have a sound board, but WordPerfect doesn't see it. Use the Sound Setup option in the Sound Clip option box to tell WordPerfect what kind of hardware you have.

You Know You're Really in Trouble When . . .

Your computer locks at startup

What's this kind of information doing in a graphics and sound chapter? You'll know the answer if you add a sound board and your computer locks. Don't panic — computers often have a hard time adjusting to new equipment. First, call whoever installed the equipment for you. Next, enlist the help of a friendly witch doctor, too (if they are not the same person). Chances are, you've got some kind of conflict problem that happens when your sound board driver loads. And for future reference (and perhaps for some help sooner than that), get a copy of Andy Rathbone's *Upgrading & Fixing PCs For Dummies* to help make sense of nonsensical hardware issues.

You've just started using Graphics mode when your cursor disappears

Did you press Home? That freezes the cursor. Your cursor may have frozen in the Off position. Press any key and your cursor should renew its happy blinking.

Man, what a weird dream?

Chapter 8 Persistent Printing

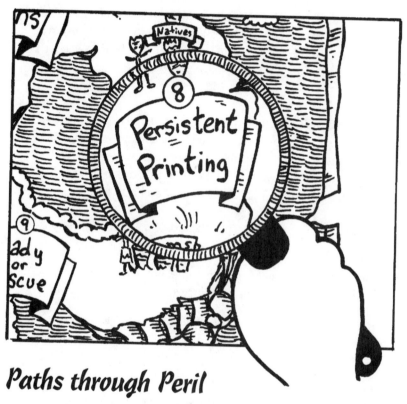

Paths through Peril

As if it weren't tough enough trying to get your message *into* the bottle, first you have to wrestle the darn thing *out* of the printer! Don't worry — with this chapter in hand, you're ready to whip most any ornery printer (laser or otherwise) and give your fax modem a good flying tackle, too. Now if you could just find a wide-mouth bottle with a good lid.

It Printeth Not, Sire!

Poison: You tried to print, but nothing came out. It's as if your printer is ignoring you — just the kind of attitude you need from a mere peripheral.

Antidote: WordPerfect is almost helpful with problems like this one (kinda scary, isn't it?). You can find potential clues in the Control Printer dialog box. To get to the dialog box, select File, Print/Fax, Control Printer from the menu or press Shift-F7, C. WordPerfect gives its view of the problem in the Message section of the dialog box and attempts to give helpful advice on resolving the problem in the Action section. If WordPerfect doesn't think anything is wrong, skip to the next section of this chapter, "It's Still Not Printing."

Note: Remember that both the problem and suggested actions are described from your program's point of view — and simple software can comprehend just so much of the real world. If your printer hops off the desk and goes cruising down the hall, WordPerfect says something like "Printer not accepting data," not "Printer making a break for it."

If WordPerfect's Action ideas don't fix the problem, consider these possibilities:

- *Is the printer on?* It's an obvious question, but that's what I get paid to ask. Make sure that the printer is plugged in to the computer, too.

- *Is the printer on-line?* Look for an on-line light or other indicator and make sure that it's lit or indicating. If it isn't, push the On-Line button (assuming that you have one).

- *Is the printer cable plugged in tightly?* Check both the computer and printer ends. Also make sure that the cable isn't stretched taut. There should be some slack — though not necessarily enough to play jump rope.

- *Is there paper in the printer?* If you're using continuous paper, also check the paper's path from "the stack" to the printer to make sure that no cables or dust bunnies are obstructing things.

- *Can you print from DOS?* Quit WordPerfect (save your document first!) and type COPY C:\AUTOEXEC.BAT LPT1: (assuming that your

printer is on the first parallel port, LPT1). Does anything print? If you use a laser printer, do any lights come on? (Laser printer note: press On-Line, Form Feed, and On-Line again to print out the page.) If nothing is happening, call your witch doctor; you've got a bonafide problem.

Is the printer beeping or flashing a light at you? Such a signal indicates that your printer is having some kind of personal problem. See the printer's manual for help or call the witch doctor.

It's Still Not Printing (but WordPerfect Doesn't Know)

Poison: *That device* still isn't printing, but everything seems fine on the surface. The right lights are on and no error messages appear in the Control Printer dialog box. But something bad is happening inside the printer, and your document is going poof! into the ether. Yet you can detect no hint of wrongdoing, no faint odor of gunpowder in the air, nothing.

Antidote: Look at your document on-screen one more time. Do you see lots of fonts and complex graphics or just a run-of-the-mill memo? If you see a simple memo, it's witch doctor time — remember to save your work before calling for help!

If your on-screen creation looks like the clip art version of a 15th-century manuscript, you may be overloading your printer's memory. This problem crops up most often with PostScript laser printers but can occur with Hewlett-Packards and compatibles as well. Hewlett-Packard printers usually try to tell you that something's wrong. PostScript printers, on the other hand, don't like to show weakness, so they usually don't print error messages.

Either way, try simplifying your document: Cut down on the number of fonts, reduce the sizes, delete some graphics. Then try printing again. If it still doesn't work, you have my personal permission to lightly smack the printer with your hand while intoning the sacred mantra, "Stupid Printer." When you're done, call the witch doctor.

There must be some way to get people's attention . . . .

It's Printing, but What?!?

Poison: Everything looked great in Print Preview, but the stuff coming out of the printer defies rational explanation.

Antidote: First, make sure that you have the right printer driver installed. Open the Print/Fax dialog box by selecting File, Print/Fax from the menu or pressing Shift-F7. Does the printer named under Current Printer look familiar? If some fiend changed the printer, click on the Select button or press S. Then choose the appropriate printer from the list (if your printer isn't listed, refer to Chapter 1 for information on how to install new printer drivers). After WordPerfect reformats your document, things should work better.

If the right printer driver was already installed, your printer cable may be bad. No, I don't understand how things that are made of metal and plastic and just lie there all day can go bad, but I know that they sometimes do. Try swapping your cable with another one that you know works. If that solves the problem, get a new cable.

If the cable is OK, and the right driver was selected, try reinstalling the printer driver. Refer to Chapter 1 and go through the printer driver installation steps. Then try printing again.

If Murphy is your officemate on this project, and none of the solutions fix the problem, you may have a more technical issue. Call your local witch doctor and hope for the best.

A Jammin' Printer

Poison: Almost every time you print, the paper jams. And jams again. And again.

Antidote: This problem usually means one of two things. Either your printer is dirty and needs to be cleaned, or your paper supply is having a crisis of some kind. Look for these possible culprits:

🔊 *Is the printer dirty?* If you open the printer's lid and see paper dust everywhere, the printer may simply need a good cleaning. If it's a dot-matrix printer, you can do the job yourself with a small vacuum cleaner. If you have a laser printer, ask the witch doctor to suggest a competent maintenance provider.

🔊 *Is the paper crooked or crinkled?* Continuous form paper must feed straight into the printer. If it doesn't, you'll get marvelously consistent jams. Single-sheet laser paper can be crooked, too. Take out the paper tray and make sure that the paper is sitting straight and flat. Also, some printers don't like you to reuse pages that printed out blank; environmentally speaking, it's a great idea, but your printer may disagree.

🔊 *Is the paper stuck together?* When refilling a laser printer paper tray, fan the paper before putting it in the tray. Hold the paper in one hand and flip through it with the other (just like when you're cruising through a *National Enquirer* in the checkout line trying to find the sea monster pictures).

🔊 *Is the printer due for a service call?* If all else fails, ask your witch doctor whether it's time for a maintenance call. Sometimes you just have to show printers how much they're loved.

It's Printing "Lite"

Poison: All your text and graphics print, but the document is very light in some areas and dark in others.

Antidote: Did you put in a new ribbon or toner cartridge lately? If you can't remember the last time you did so, it's probably "that time" again. Call your witch doctor if you're unsure about the procedure.

If you're getting the light-and-dark problem, particularly with a laser printer, try removing the toner cartridge. (If you don't know what a toner cartridge is, don't try this by yourself — get some help.) Gently shake the cartridge back and forth to disperse the toner evenly in the cartridge. Put the cartridge back in the printer and try printing again. But remember to put in a new cartridge soon; light-and-dark printing is a sure sign that you're running low on toner.

It's Verrry Sllooowww

Poison: Everything looks great once your document is printed, but (gadzooks!) the printer is taking its sweet time about delivering pages.

Antidote: You're probably experiencing a memory problem. If your computer has only 1MB of RAM, WordPerfect prints like molasses in winter. It takes so long to print a page, in fact, that if you look up "slow" in the dictionary, you just may find a reference to WordPerfect printing on your computer. Depressing, isn't it?

The solution is easy enough — as are all things when you have the right resources. Give your computer more RAM. If you can't do that, reorganize your work schedule so that you have some small, mindless tasks to do while waiting for your printouts. Alas.

If memory isn't the issue, look at the document again. If it's particularly large or contains a wide variety of art or graphic fonts, it will print slowly — such is the nature of these things. You can speed the process up by reducing the number of fonts, changing to an internal printer font, or cutting down on the pretty pictures.

That's Not the Font I Had in Mind

Poison: Despite your best efforts, your printer refuses to use the font that you specified in the document. Instead, it substitutes Courier for Trunkleberry Gothic Bold — and Courier, for goodness sake, doesn't match the mood of your prose *at all*.

Antidote: Fear not, brave adventurer! Everyone wrestles with this problem at one time or another. Some specific things to look for include:

- *If the printer is ignoring the initial font you set, turn on Reveal Codes (select View, Reveal Codes or press Alt-F3) and look for any other font code.* In WordPerfect, codes in the document override the initial font choice.

- *Make sure that you selected the right printer.* Each printer can have a different initial font, so check whether you're using a printer that has the initial font you want.

Techie Term

Unlike typewriters and dot-matrix printers, which use inked ribbons, laser printers use plastic "ink" called *toner.* During printing, the printer lays the toner onto the page and then melts it into the paper (that's why laser-printed pages are warm when they come out of the printer). Be careful not to spill any toner when you change your printer's toner cartridge because toner stains are usually permanent on clothes and carpeting. (Sorry — but at least now you know that those slacks really *are* ruined.)

If you're having trouble printing a graphics font, check the Location of Files setting and make sure that it's pointing to the right subdirectory. Select File, Setup, Location of Files, Graphic Fonts Data Files. WordPerfect displays the entries for all available font types. If you don't know which type of font you're using (or wouldn't know a correct directory entry if it ran up and bit you), consult your witch doctor for help.

Run the Font Installer program (select Font, Font, Setup or press Ctrl-F8, Shift-F1) and make sure that WordPerfect understands that the fonts you have on disk are the ones that you want to use when printing. In this crazy world of flying data chunks, programs can forget such trivial details. (No, I don't know why.)

For more information
about fonts, fonting, and
(my favorite tense) "will have
been being fonted," refer to Chapter 6.

Let's Line Up There!

Poison: Columns of text don't line up on the page but look fine on-screen.

Antidote: If you're using a proportional font (just about anything *other* than Courier) and manually creating columns of text, you have to use tabs to line up your words. If you try to use spaces like you did in the good old days — when *word processing* meant *typing* and "Selectric" came after "IBM" — things will look OK on-screen but absolutely awful on paper. Take the time to learn about tabs. If you're trying to do something particularly intricate, submit yourself to the pain of tables. You can find marvelous, patient explanations for both of these features in IDG's *WordPerfect 6 For Dummies.*

If you're using a table or tabs and you can't get your columns to print correctly, your document may contain some spaces or funky codes. Use Reveal Codes (select View, Reveal Codes or press Alt-F3) to sleuth the perpetrator. If further investigation turns up nothing suspicious, call in Sherlock witch doctor for an in-depth consultation.

Bad (Page) Breaks

Poison: You print the final, glorious copy of your 30-page masterwork and notice a teeny-tiny (but very important) error on page 4. Being the diligent type, you correct the error and add some brief, overlooked explanations with it. When you reprint page 4, you find that the text isn't all there; some slid over to page 5, which lost some to page 6, and so on.

Antidote: Even modest corrections to an already-printed document can cause this scenario. The extra material that you added caused your page break to move, which in turn moved the break on the following page and the one after that, and the one after that, and the one . . . you get the idea. Here are your options:

> *Remove the extra text, leaving just the correction that you went in to make in the first place.* Granted, this compromise throws away the valuable additional thoughts you recorded in your prize-winning epoch, but it *does* get the darn thing out the door without waiting for a complete reprint.

> *Look for a nearby page that's partially empty and ends in a hard page break.* If you find one, reprint from your corrected page through the "short" page. Because the short page wasn't full to begin with (hey — no brain power required for that one), the material you added will hopefully just make it a "medium page." The hard page break insulates the rest of your document from your current gyrations, so the other umpteen pages should be fine.

🔊 *Try inserting a hard page break to make the text wrap the way you want.* Position your cursor where you want the break and select Layout, Alignment, Hard Page or press Ctrl-Enter. Because WordPerfect already believes that the text won't fit on one page, this command may not work. If your document is especially long or complex, though, it may be worth a try.

🔊 *Give in and reprint the whole document.* Sure, your friends from "Save A Tree In Rural Environments" would hate you if they knew, but who's going to tell?

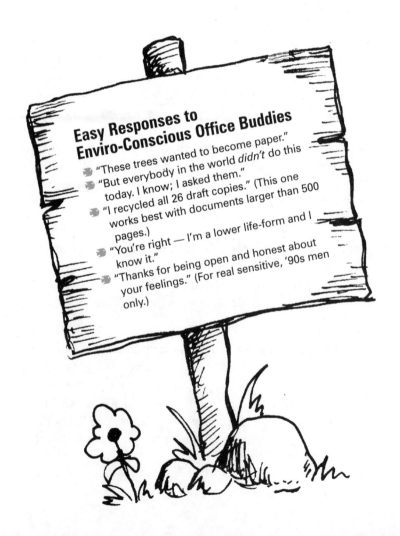

Easy Responses to Enviro-Conscious Office Buddies

🔊 "These trees wanted to become paper."

🔊 "But everybody in the world *didn't* do this today. I know; I asked them."

🔊 "I recycled all 26 draft copies." (This one works best with documents larger than 500 pages.)

🔊 "You're right — I'm a lower life-form and I know it."

🔊 "Thanks for being open and honest about your feelings." (For real sensitive, '90s men only.)

WordPerfect Doesn't See My Fax Modem

Poison: After you spent all that money on a super-cool fax modem, WordPerfect won't let you use the thing. The Fax Service line in the Print/Fax dialog box isn't available. Oh, nuts.

Antidote: It sounds as if WordPerfect just doesn't know there's a fax modem out there. The answer to this situation is (gulp!) back at the DOS prompt (fade up eerie organ music).

1. **Save your document and quit WordPerfect.** At the DOS prompt (C:\>), type TYPE \AUTOEXEC.BAT and press Enter. Look for two entries that mention FAXDIR and FAXB (if you have certain models of Intel SatisFAXtion fax modems, you'll see CASMGR and INTELFAX instead). These programs help WordPerfect send faxes. Because they're in your AUTOEXEC.BAT file, they should load every time you start your computer. If they're not in the file, it could be why your fax modem isn't working. Contact your witch doctor or the WordPerfect help line for assistance.

2. **Make sure that your copy of WordPerfect was set up for faxing.** Type DIR/S \WP60\FAX*.* (DIR/S \INTELFAX*.* for Intel SatisFAXtion owners) and press Enter. DOS should list several files, including the FAXDIR.EXE and FAXB.COM programs. If you don't see the files, WordPerfect probably isn't fax-ready yet.

3. **If everything looks right, make sure that your fax modem is turned on and connected to your computer.** Double-check your modem cable; try a modem cable that you know is OK. Reboot your machine (Ctrl-Alt-Delete) and carefully watch the screen as the system starts. Look for error messages when FAXDIR and FAXB (or the SatisFAXtion software) loads.

4. **Even if FAXDIR and FAXB load correctly, you still may have specified the wrong COM (short for "communications") port for your modem.** In the CAS Setup Utility (\WP60\SETUP.EXE), choose option 2 (Hardware driver setup). The first option on the screen is the COM port. Press the spacebar to toggle through the options. Most

modems are attached to either COM1 or COM2, so try those settings first. Press F10 a few times to save your changes, reboot your machine, and try WordPerfect again. If neither the COM1 nor COM 2 setting works, try COM3 and COM4.

5. **If all else fails, call your witch doctor or WordPerfect product support — not only will these folks be sympathetic, they may even be able to help.**

Tip: If you're planning on doing a lot of faxing, be sure to get the Version 6.0A update of WordPerfect. It has some expanded faxing services as well as other "feature enhancements" (read "bug fixes").

Fax Locks Up System; Film at 11:00

Poison: Sometimes when you fax things, the system locks up. You don't get an error message — maybe the system doesn't have time before paralysis sets in — your computer just goes clunk.

Antidote: Because this whole fax thing is driven by TSRs (terminate-and-stay-resident programs), it's predisposed to peril. TSRs are the bane of the

Techie Term

A *fax modem* is a marvelous thing. It's part data modem (for calling CompuServe, Prodigy, and other on-line services) and part fax machine (the sending and receiving part, not the printing part — that's why you have a printer). With a fax modem attached to your computer, you can type a memo in WordPerfect, create a cover sheet, and then say, "WordPerfect, fax this!" If you're looking for a fax modem, some good brands are Intel, Hayes, and Practical Peripherals.

Words of Wisdom: Making a Fax Modem Work with WordPerfect

Depending on your specific fax modem, WordPerfect needs two TSRs (terminate-and-stay-resident programs) to make the process work. In fact, if WordPerfect doesn't see those two TSRs in memory when it starts, it assumes that you don't have a fax modem and disables the fax option entirely.

When you're setting up WordPerfect, it gives you the opportunity to install the fax software. The program provides different options for different kinds of modems, so if you're not sure which setting matches your system, consult your fax modem's documentation or manufacturer or ask your witch doctor.

Regardless of what software was included with the fax modem, if you want to fax *directly* from WordPerfect's Print/Fax menu, you must install and configure WordPerfect's fax options. The process is fraught with technical pitfalls, so this might be a good time to buy some munchies and have your witch doctor over for a "just the fax (modem)" configuration party.

computer world. For the most part, they aren't used any more except for things like faxing. Hmpf.

It's likely that something is arguing with the fax TSRs (like another TSR, perhaps?). The result: Your system shuts down to watch the fight. If you use DOS 5 or earlier and Intel SatisFAXtion, call your witch doctor for help.

If you use DOS 6, try rebooting and pressing F5 when the words `Starting MS-DOS...` appear on-screen. This action prompts a "clean boot" of your computer — the system skips everything in your CONFIG.SYS and AUTOEXEC.BAT files and uses a simple, default setup. Manually load the fax programs (type CD \WP60, FAXDIR, FAXB). Start WordPerfect and try faxing a document. If the system still locks up, it's witch doctor time.

It's Not Dialing Right

Poison: The fax modem works great up to the point when it has to dial the phone. You hear it start to dial, but after it dials 9 for an outside line, the dial tone doesn't come right back. The modem blithely keeps on dialing

through the silence, so the rest of the number is lost. Can't the thing even dial a phone correctly?

Antidote: You can use an old witch doctor trick to solve this problem. When you need to dial 9 (or some other number) to get an outside line, put a comma (,) after the 9. The comma tells the modem to pause a moment before continuing to dial, giving the phone system time to get the outside dial tone. For example, 9,555-4357 instructs the modem to dial 9, wait a second or two, and then dial 555-4357. If your phone system still needs more time before dialing the number, put in more than one comma.

Reading Smoke Signals

Printer not accepting data

You'll find this message cowering in the Control Printer dialog box; it doesn't come out and chase you. The message means that for one reason or another, your printer isn't listening to WordPerfect. See the section "It Printeth Not, Sire!" earlier in this chapter for trouble-shooting help.

Error (11): Fax Modem Not Responding, Check Hardware

This error message comes from FAXDIR, so you may not notice it until WordPerfect won't give you access to fax services. Check the COM port setting in the

Insufficient memory

No Fax Capability

Fax Not Responding

Printer not accepting data

SETUP program (and look at the "WordPerfect Doesn't See My Fax Modem" section in this chapter).

Error (12): Modem Does Not Have Fax Capabilities Or Wrong Fax Modem Type

Here's another error message that will send you back to the SETUP program. Fax modems come in different types: Class 1, Class 2, and CAS are the main delineations. You see this error message if the wrong modem type is selected during setup. For example, if FAXDIR thinks that you have a Class 1 modem and tries Class 1-style communication, the modem basically says, "Ummmm, uh, what?" in response. Try changing the modem type to one of the other options.

Unable to access client F (EF) ',0
Insufficient cache memory
Insufficient memory

All three of these messages relate to printing or faxing with low conventional memory (the 640K part of your computer's memory). If WordPerfect doesn't have a full 470K (or, better yet, 530K) of conventional memory available when it loads, you're likely to receive one of these pleasant tokens of its esteem. If the problem occurs right after you load your fax modem software for the first time, you've found the likely culprit. Don't worry, though — a good witch doctor can help you find extra memory on your system (provided you have DOS 5 or 6) and make everything work better. In the meantime, save your work often and create two plain documents in the morning (my bill will be in the mail).

You Know You're Really in Trouble When . . .

Every time you try to print, your system locks up

The problem could be a software fight, but it's more likely to be a hardware issue. Try a clean boot (users up to DOS 5, boot with your System Survival Disk; DOS 6 users, reboot and press F5 when you see Starting MS-DOS...). Start WordPerfect and try printing. If the system *still* locks up, make backup copies of anything you care about and call your witch doctor pronto.

You can fax fine all year long, except in July

I know you think I'm kidding, but this is an actual problem.

If you have an Intel SatisFAXtion modem that suddenly won't fax on July 1, you need a new copy of a file called INTELFAX.COM. Your version likes to do the summer vacation thing that month, so faxing is out of the question. The updated version is more of a workaholic and will take care of the problem. The INTELFAX.COM update is available directly from Intel. Get your witch doctor to help, just in case you're really dealing with some other wacky glitch of summer.

Tip: If you really *are* having the July failure, try this short-term fix: go back to DOS and change the system date to something other than July. (Type DATE and enter a new date when the system prompts you to do so.) Poof! Because it isn't July anymore, your computer should fax now. This is *not* a permanent fix; by all means, get the updated INTELFAX.COM file from Intel — and remember to change the date back!

Chapter 9

Ready for Rescue: Manic Merging

Paths through Peril

That angry-looking
native with the razor-
sharp spear is not a
welcome sight. Nor is
the wild boar snorting
just beyond the under-
brush. Hey, wait a
minute — maybe you
should just step back
quietly and let them . . .
merge.

Mixed-Up Data

Poison: Merged in the wrong places

You created and saved your form file, and you created and saved your data file. When you ran the merge, everything seemed to go without a hitch. But when the documents appear on-screen, the data has been plugged into all the wrong places.

Antidote: Display the data file and read through the FIELDNAMES row. Are the field names entered in the right order? Now look through your data entries. Did you transpose a field or two as you were entering data? WordPerfect will go right through the list and plug whatever data's there into the available slot. It won't look at the ZIP code and think, "Hmmm, the word *Frank* shouldn't go in ZIP code!" Make sure that the entries in your data file match the order in the FIELDNAMES row. Use the prompt at the bottom of the screen to help you figure out which field the cursor is currently highlighting.

Disappearing Fields

Poison: Missing in inaction

Techie Term

If you are sending your mailing to one hundred people, you need a *form file* (or the document which you plug data into) and a *data file* (which contains the data regarding the hundred people.)

Fields are areas in the form file into which data is plugged. Instead of "Dear So-and-So," for example, your form file would include "Dear FIELD(Firstname)". When you merge the form file with the data file, the data from the Firstname field is substituted in FIELD(Firstname)'s place.

After you run the merge (by opening the Tools menu and choosing Merge, Run) you see that all the data appears except one field, which just isn't there.

Antidote: WordPerfect is very particular about the way you enter field names. The field names on the data file and the form file must match exactly (not including capitalization). If you add an extra space or misspell a file name, WordPerfect won't know what to do with the data. Take a look at the FIELDNAME line in your data file to make sure that the field names there match the field names in your form file. If there's a mistake in the FIELDNAME line, edit it as you would any other document text.

Let's See . . . What D'ya Call That?

Poison: Field name forgetfulness

OK, so WordPerfect wants you to be exact in the way you enter the field names. But how do you remember every single field?

Antidote: You don't have to rely on memory (or even scribbled notes) to tell you how to spell your field names. WordPerfect 6's List Field Names option enables you to look at what you've done before you create the data form.

The problem is that you have to set up your data file before you create the form in order to benefit from the field list. Create

the data file and save it. When you want to add the fields to the form, choose Field in the Merge Codes (Form File) dialog box. When the Parameter Entry box appears, click on List Field Names. Then enter the name of the data file that you created and press Enter. The field names appear in the list.

Note: The easiest way to see both the data file and the form file is to display them both on-screen at once. Make sure that both files are open and then choose Window, Tile.

How to Recycle Merge Forms

After you create a merge document or two, you should see a certain pattern developing. The same fields appear in similar documents. In a personal merge letter, for example, you may have first and last name, address, kid's names (for the line "How are FIELD(kid1) and FIELD(kid2)?"). For a business document, you would have customer first and last name, business name, address, city, state, ZIP, phone, fax . . . all that good stuff.

Why create the same layout over and over again every time you do a merge print project? You can save the basic layout of your merge data form and reuse it, saving time, trouble, and probably electricity.

After you've finished a merge project, make a copy of the data form (you may want to delete the project-specific information first and just leave the field names) and use the Save As command to save it out to disk under a unique name. Name it something like HOLIDAY.MRG or CLIENT.MRG so that you'll remember what it is for.

If you do quite a bit of merging (lucky you), you may want to create a directory just to store merge data forms and data files. For information on creating a directory from within WordPerfect, see the sidebar "How to Manage Files and Directories" in Chapter 4.

Turning a Document into a Form Letter

Poison: Dual-life text

You created this great sales letter. Everyone said that it was terrific. You decided that you finally hit upon the perfect sales tool. How can you turn this single document into a form letter so that hundreds of clients can fall victim to the pull of your marketing prowess?

Antidote: You can easily turn a favorite document into a form file. First, save the document by using the Save As command; name it something like FORMLET.MRG so that you'll remember later what you plan to do with it. Then open this newly created file and replace the typed data with the variable fields. Say the opening looks like

> Matthew Hawthorne
> 23 Westkirk Rd.
> Columbus, IN 47201

You delete "Matthew," and with the cursor still positioned where the first name was, open the Tools menu and choose Merge, Define, and Form. Then type the field name to go in place of the text (Firstname) and press Enter. The field is inserted at the cursor position.

Continue in this way until you've added the fields that you need in order to turn the document into a merge form file. Remember to save the file when you're through.

Moving On Up!

Poison: A few ambitious field entries

The data merged satisfactorily in most records, but a few are out of whack.

Antidote: The problem is in the data file, where one or more of the records is missing a field entry. For example, if you have your form set up like

> Firstname Lastname
> Title
> Company
> Address
> City, State ZIP

There he is!
Hey, Witch Doctor
— over here!

and one of your clients doesn't list a Title, your data will look like

> Bob Baxter
>
> Baxter's Bakery
> 23 Bluebird Blvd.
> Bingham, MA 01965

The blank is natural — WordPerfect is expecting data for that slot. But if you don't do something in the data file (and that something is press F9 to add an ENDFIELD code), the Company data will move up to fill the Title field, and the Address data will move up to fill the Company field, and so on. And then you'll have a mess.

To correct this problem, return to the data file and find the offending record. At the point that causes everything to go crazy, position the cursor and press F9. This command inserts an ENDFIELD code, telling WordPerfect that there is no value in the field. WordPerfect skips to the next field and puts the right data in the right place.

Now resave the file and run your merge again. This time, things should look better.

Much Ado about Blank Fields

Poison: Returning the empties

You understand why your data edged up in the form letter, but what are you supposed to do about the blank fields that occur in hard-to-fix places? Like when you don't know what name to put for Firstname.

Antidote: The best solution is to copy the offending records out to a new data file (you can highlight and copy them as you would any text in the document) and then modify a copy of the original form file to better fit those records.

Words of Wisdom:

Bar Codes

WordPerfect 6.0 now makes it possible for you to add POSTNET bar codes to your envelopes or mailing labels. These bar codes make it possible for postal scanners to sort letters according to ZIP code. To add a bar code, put the cursor where you want the code to appear, open the Layout menu, and choose Other, Bar Code. Then type the ZIP code (9 or 11 digits, with or without hyphens) and click on OK. You can see the code in either Graphics or Page mode.

Custom Labels

Although WordPerfect supplies definitions for many commonly used labels, it's unrealistic to think that these definitions could cover all possibilities. If you've got a label that defies definition, you can define it yourself by selecting Layout, Page, Labels.

WordPerfect's Merge Programming Language

A merge operation that requires its own programming language must be pretty complicated. Nevertheless, WordPerfect includes a set of commands that you can use to insert various programming features in your form file. You may never use this language, but it's nice to know that it's there.

Note: If you want to remove the blank lines that are left when there's no entry for a field, open the Tools menu, choose Merge, select Run, and change the setting in Blank Fields in Data File to Remove Resulting Blank Line.

Out, Standing in the Field

Poison: Can't keep fields straight

Your form file has so many fields that you're having an awful time entering the data correctly in the data file. Isn't there any safety feature to alert you when you're entering data in the wrong place?

Wow. These guys are always so sentimental. The natives have built another monument in your honor.

Antidote: If the loose style of the data file doesn't suit you, try the more structured table file. The field names stretch across the top of table; after you make your entry, you press Tab to move from field to field. That way, it's easy to see whether you miss one.

Jumbled Merge Table Text

Poison: What does that *say?*

But just *look* at those columns! Each column is only three characters wide. The word *Company* stretches over three lines.

Uh, oh! Not another tidal wave! Be careful — don't fall overboard!

Antidote: The Table Edit commands in the Merge Codes (Table Data File) dialog box allow you to add and delete rows and columns in the table. Remove anything that you really don't need and then use Layout Tables Edit to change the width of the columns (select the column and press Ctrl-right arrow to widen or Ctrl-left arrow to shorten).

Merge-Printing Fields Forever

Poison: Too many codes

You're tired of looking at the ENDFIELD and ENDRECORD codes. Is there any way to hide them?

Antidote: Open the Tools menu, choose Merge, and select Define. In the Display of Merge Codes section, you can select either Show Codes as Icons or Hide Codes.

Off-the-Edge Labels

Poison: Botched label printing

You thought that this label thing would be a breeze. You chose the label type and started the merge print. The text starts printing before it gets to the edge of the label.

Antidote: Don't expect label printing to go smoothly right from the beginning. So much of getting labels to print properly has to do with their alignment in the printer. If the labels are too high or too low, try adjusting the platen so that the print head is positioned where you want the first line of text to begin. For best results, do a couple of test prints (print just a few labels) before launching into a complete data file.

If the text is printing off the edges of the label because the label definition is too large, choose a different label definition or edit the current one by selecting Format, Page, Labels, Edit.

Half-Hearted Labels

Poison: Half-here, half-gone

You got the labels to work with the merge operation. Everything looked fine. But when the printer spit out the labels, the printing on some was cut off.

Antidote: All the label settings in WordPerfect's Predefined Labels file are set to have 0" label margins, meaning that the printing goes all the way to the edge of the page. Most laser printers, however, have an unprintable margin (varying from .25 to .5, depending on the printer), and your laser printer won't print in this area. You can try changing the label type (some are made specifically for laser printers with print boundaries) or create your own custom label definition — or give up and look for someone's unused dot-matrix printer.

Oh, no! Where did the witch doctor go now?

Molasseslike Merging

Poison: Slow-moving merge

Merge is going very slowly. You've been amusing yourself as much as possible, but your frustration is rising precariously to screaming level.

Antidote: Mail merging — and merge printing — are two operations that require quite a bit of data processing from WordPerfect. And if you've sorted the records or asked WordPerfect to print only those that meet a certain criterion, you're pushing RAM even more to the max. If your merge is taking longer than expected, check the following factors:

- *Are you using WordPerfect 5.1 files?* If you are, WordPerfect 6.0 is converting the files as it merges them. Save time by opening the files in 6.0 and saving them before doing the merge.

- *Do you have graphics in the files?* If so, double-click on the image(s) and change the Content setting to Image on Disk. This procedure removes the graphic from the document but leaves a pointer telling WordPerfect to look for it on the disk that you specify, thus freeing up more RAM.

🐦 *Are you using search and sort features?* If you can, skip the fancy stuff and do a straight merge — just mix the data file with the form file. This straightforward process is much easier for WordPerfect to do and requires less processing time.

If you've checked these things and nothing seems to be helping, call your witch doctor for further advice on streamlining your merge procedure.

Reading Smoke Signals

Things are confusing enough when it comes to mail merging; you probably won't have the chance to fret over error messages. Here, nonetheless, are a couple that you may see:

File not found

If you haven't saved your data file or form file under the name that you thought you used, WordPerfect isn't going to be able to find the file at merge time (hence, the error message). Click on OK to get beyond the message and use the File Manager to determine where, exactly, you saved that file. Or, if the file is one of the last four you've used, you can select it by clicking the down arrow beside the Form File or Data File options.

No Envelopes Defined

You're trying to merge print envelopes and you haven't created an envelope definition yet. Do so by opening the

Format menu, choosing Envelope, and entering the necessary settings for the return and mailing addresses.

You Know You're Really in Trouble When . . .

You didn't save your data file changes

Mail merge is particularly confusing because you can have so many different files open at one time. You may have a data file, a form file, and the recently created merge file — which you are now about to update by editing the data file. Get it? Lots of possibilities for trouble. Keep your files straight and save them every time you change something. For really important data files — ones that will take you more than a few minutes to type back in — get in the habit of saving them out to disk and storing them in their own little disk holder.

You printed a hundred envelopes with the return address and mailing address mixed up

It's a hard lesson, but we all learn it sooner or later. Do a test print — especially when you're working with mail merge. In other words, don't cross your fingers and hope that the addresses come out where they should; instead, print one envelope and check to make sure everything's OK. If something's wrong, correct the problem. Reprinting one envelope is a great deal less hassle (and embarrassment) than reprinting a hundred.

Epilogue

Oh, the stories you'll have to tell when this experience is over. They'll be boring grandchildren for generations to come. Twenty years from now, your WordPerfect-wrestling feats will seem incredible. When multimedia, neural networks, and virtual reality fall by the wayside, all to be replaced by a brand of technology that we can now only imagine.

But there will always be witch doctors.

And there will always be those of us who feel stranded — cast away — by the rapid pace of it all, thrown into some kind of high-tech rat race with time. Sometimes, it's by choice, but too often all of this technology is imposed upon us. And in a sea of company procedure, policy, and politics, we are somehow left alone. Yes, set adrift in a sea of technology, with the human element distinctly no where to be found.

Take heart, though, because things have a way of coming around again. The pendulum swings this way and that. But it always comes back again. This week you'll be learning WordPerfect, and next week it'll be Excel. Tomorrow, who knows? But this much is for certain: There will always be folks who are willing to help each other — through it all.

An *S.O.S.* book may get you through this time, but don't worry, you'll find your own witch doctors. In the meantime, I've gathered together some advice from some of the best that we were able to track down. Sure, it's kind of general and philosophical, and it may not seem to relate to your problems much right now; but you'd be surprised. These are the secrets that every good witch doctor abides by. Study them. Learn to feel them, live them, breathe them.

There are at least a few of you out there who someday are going to be witch doctors, too. (Don't laugh; I'm not kidding.)

When Should You Call the Witch Doctor?

This is a personal decision. The range of choices runs from anytime to never. Take your pick. I'd say that it's safe to say that when you've run out of possibilities of your own for solving a problem, it's probably a good time to start.

Beyond that, think about the costs and benefits. State-of-the-art advice can be very expensive, and free advice can turn out to be very expensive, too. The most important thing you can do is become a proactive learner of the technology that confronts you. Apparently, you are, or you wouldn't be here. So, congratulations. I think you're on the right track.

So, What Do the Scrolls Mean?

I thought you'd ask. Here's what all of those hints were about in the DOS Island journey. Again, study them. A little troubleshooting theory isn't going to kill you.

Isolate the problem

Isolating the problem means finding what's *really* wrong. Many times, the surface symptom ("I just turned it on and it said 'Non-system disk or disk error.' Is my hard drive gone?") may or may not be the ultimate problem ("Hey! Who left this floppy disk in my computer?"). The trick to troubleshooting is finding and fixing *problems*, not *symptoms*. It's a process. One step and then another. Change one thing, try again. Pick a spot and troubleshoot in one direction. Isolate the problem and then solve it. One trick is to follow the power source. Follow the path of electricity. Follow the path of information. Rule out possible causes each step along the way.

Start Over and Try Again

The simplest case is: Turn it off. Wait a few seconds. Turn it back on. And try again. You would be amazed how may times this works. Who cares why. It just does.

When you have a problem. Go back to the beginnning. Retrace your steps. Things may not be as they had seemed when you first got into the mess.

Always Have a Backup

There's an old computer saying that goes like this: "There are two kinds of people in the world: those whose hard drives have failed on them and those whose haven't — yet." It's a real gem, isn't it? The saying is very true (everyone who's lost a drive is sagely nodding right now). If you're one of the lucky ones whose drive is still running, *now* is the time to learn about backups. Start today, right now, this minute — before it's too late.

Many application programs have an "autosave" feature which helps when you're deeply focused on "creating" and kinda-sorta forgot to save that document you just worked on all morning. If you've got this option, use it! Startup disks are something else you just can't have enough of. You should have at least one (preferably two) System Survival Disks handy at all times. Back up your passwords, too. If you're working with password-protected files, seal your password in an envelope and give it to your boss or other trusted coworker.

The simplest data backups involve copying things to floppy disks as you create them. For example, when you finish a document in your word processor, take a second and use the Save As command (or whatever it is in your particular package) to put a copy on a diskette. Save the original on the hard drive. To make the data *much* safer, take the disk home with you each night and bring it back the following day. Backups don't do much good if they're sitting next to the computer while the building burns down around them.

More complex and larger backups usually require extra accessories for your computer. The most common item is a tape backup system. It's common to use more than one tape when you back up this way. With two tapes, you'd use Tape #1 this week and Tape #2 next week. The third week, go back to Tape #1. This way, you always have a backup for your backup.

Backups are funny things. If you never need them, dealing with them seems like more of a pain than it's worth. When the time comes (and it will), you'll look like a hero. Put some serious time and effort into designing a backup system for your computer. If your PC is your lifeblood, find a witch doctor to get you set up. Remember that you're doing this for yourself — a backup is personal insurance that *will* pay off; the only question is when.

Know How to Undo Things

So here you are: something bad happened and you want to go back in time to the point before whatever-it-is went wrong. In short, you want to *undo* the crisis. Undo is one of those techno-philosophical concepts that keeps many nerds going at 3 a.m. and many Chinese restaurants flush with late-night business.

Depending on your situation, "undo" can have many forms. Conceptually, you're trying to reverse or otherwise bail out of a bad situation. Here are some ideas to get you out of whatever dire straights you've gotten yourself into:

➧ *Keep a current backup.* A good backup is the ultimate "undo."

➧ *Quit without saving.* Almost every program known to mankind has an almost neurotic desire to save your changes. What if you don't *want* to save them? Close the file or quit the program. When it asks if you want to save those all-important changes, say no. Voilà! You're right back to where you started.

🐭 *Try Undo.* The Undo command traditionally lets you escape the consequences of whatever heinous software crime you've committed, but ONLY your most recent one. Multiple heinous software crimes are beyond the forgiving capacities of Undo; seek solace from Quit without Saving.

🐭 *Escape, Ctrl-C, and Ctrl-Break.* These are DOS-level tricks (although Escape often works in application programs too!). If you typed FORMAT C: just to see what it looked like sitting there on the command line and are now too terrified to move, press any of these keys. They tell DOS to ignore what's on the command line (Escape) or stop whatever it's trying to do right now (Ctrl-C or Ctrl-Break). By the way, they're in order by strength. Often, Ctrl-Break will get you out of a bind that the other two won't seem to affect.

🐭 *Beware of programs that make changes for you.* Many installation routines "help" you by posting changes to your CONFIG.SYS and AUTOEXEC.BAT files (and WIN.INI for Windows programs). Granted, they usually warn you of what they're about to do, but it's still not the same as a qualified witch doctor inserting the same changes. If things don't work right after the automated surgery, look for the backup copies of these files.

🐭 *Look for automatic .BAK files.* Some programs (such as Microsoft Word) automatically make backup files for you.

Don't Make Assumptions

Believe it or not, this is what separates decent troubleshooters from Great Witch Doctors. If you master it, it will have the same effect on your computing future. When you're trying to resolve something, watch out for your assumptions. Like blinders that limit your vision, they can send you off on wild-goose chases, snipe hunts, Congressional fact-finding junkets, and

other wastes of time. Incorrect assumptions can even *prevent* you from finding the correct answer. How do you avoid this?

🔖 *Don't get focused on "the answer" too soon.* Sometimes a problem appears that you've dealt with before. You immediately implement your tried-and-true solution, which doesn't work this time. After spending time and effort chasing an assumed problem, you've still got the real problem left to solve. Using previous experience is vital, but always leave your mind open to new twists on old plots.

🔖 *Separate obvious symptoms from hidden problems.* This goes back to good troubleshooting technique.

🔖 *Don't assume it's really a problem.* Many, many "problems" are solved by just turning the stupid machine off and on again. Try it. Keep in mind that the average 386 is doing a few million things *per second*. If it runs without a hitch for one minute, it's done *several hundred million* consecutive things right. If it screws up once in a while, who could blame it? Restart and then give it a chance to try again.

🔖 *Look for the right things.* If you're having an "I've lost something" crisis, don't assume you're looking in the right place. Make sure you've got the right *file* in the right *directory* on the right *disk*.

🔖 *Don't assume any one step is working.* Think through the process step by step. Things you skipped because you assumed them to be correct can be your downfall. Check and then check again.

🔖 *Don't assume the blame yet; it may not be your fault.* When something in your computer does the electronic equivalent of going "ping," it's perfectly normal (if not factually correct) to blurt out "I broke it. I killed it. It's all my fault." Many times, *you* didn't break it. It just broke. Don't jump on yourself too quickly.

If you *did* do it, learn from the experience. Keep your perspective. These things are never *that* tragic — really. Don't verbally berate yourself into a high blood pressure prescription; it's just not worth it.

Don't Panic

"Format complete," the screen sadistically chirps. A thick veil lifts from your consciousness and you wonder, "Format of *what* is complete? Was I *formatting* something?!?" Your stress level begins an inexorable climb as you remember all those silly questions the computer rather unexpectedly asked you a few minutes ago (the ones like "All data will be erased. OK to proceed?" and the almighty "Are you sure?"). Did they really *mean* something? Visions flash before your eyes: spreadsheets predicting the financial future of your world, Pulitzer prize-winning justification memos, that super-cool jet fighter game with the high score in your name. Your eyes grow wide and the index finger on your left hand begins to involuntarily twitch.

This is *panic*. And panic-stricken people do not operate computers very well.

Bury what I'm about to say deep in your subconscious where it can fight its way to the surface when your brain hits the panic button: *get up and get away*. Put a little sign on the computer that says "having a bad hair day" and walk out of there for a few minutes. Get all the emotion out of your system and regain logical control before you even think about sitting down at your computer again. This *will* be hard, but you'll thank me later.

When it's time for your moment like this, remember that madly thrashing around trying to "fix" whatever crisis you're having will probably do more damage than the crisis itself entails. Almost any problem can be solved, provided a logical, rational mind is at the helm. If you think the problem is that big, call someone before you try anything. Panic throws everything out of proportion, making even the smallest of problems look like a disaster. Just go somewhere and settle down. When you're approximating normalcy again, have another look at your computer.

Think First

Don't jump wholeheartedly into the first possible solution; think about what you're doing. Sit back and *think* about the problem you want to solve.

Thinking costs nothing yet can save mondo amounts of time, effort, and psychological wear and tear. Think first before you issue that FORMAT command, before you copy that file, before you turn off your machine. Being in too much of a hurry now can cost you hours of grief later.

Write It Down

Witch doctors are part of another realm, thus error messages that look like gibberish to us might be useful to them (of course, it might be gibberish to them too, but they just don't want to tell us). Being rescued doesn't mean you couldn't have done it yourself. In fact, if you play your cards right, you *can* do it yourself next time. If you get yourself in a jam, write down the problem and how you got out of it. Then, whenever you get stuck, consult your list to see if you had the same problem before. If so, great. You can look at the steps you took last time and fix things yourself.

If not, that's okay, too. Just write down how you fix the problem this time so that next time you'll know what to do.

Be specific; don't approximate error messages. If it beeped, write down any patterns (long-short-short). If you tried solutions, write down what you did and in what order (the order is as important as what you did). Write down how you fixed it this time. Write down all the steps you went through when you created something. Write down how you answered queries. Write down what you didn't do. Very often these notes will save your neck later.

Don't Move

When you're troubleshooting, one thing often leads to another, which leads to another, and you keep digging further as you chase the elusive problem.

So many times you find a problem and think "Hey — this one'll be easy." Ultimately, you find that you've landed the Queen Mother of All Iceberg Problems. Somewhere along the way, it begins to exceed your ability; the problem begins to win. You'll raise your eyes from the morass of unplugged cables, strewn manuals, and scribbled notes. Your brain will desperately whisper, "I'm over my head. I think I'm in trouble."

Moments like this can be great learning experiences. They can also be the last moments of your computer's useful life on the planet. Knowing when to call for help is a most valuable skill in computer troubleshooting. It saves wear and tear on you, your computer, and your witch doctor.

Once you reach this point, frantically resist the urge to try "just one more thing." Witch doctors often perform miracles but (equally as often) are seriously impaired by the "last thing" their acolyte tried. If a problem is serious enough that you've given every bit of skill and daring you possess chasing it to the ground, it's also important enough to make you swallow any remaining pride and speak the words "Help me; help my computer."

Once you've given up, don't go back. If you get a brainstorm and you're *positive* this will solve the problem, write down your thoughts and sit on your hands. Discuss your idea with the witch doctor. Don't attempt the resolution again. You might be taking that last step which separates you from the digital disaster.

Don't Be Afraid

I heard someone say once that people just need to take responsibility where their computers are concerned. Keep a positive, nonintimidated attitude. Basically, be a proactive user. Take charge of your PC. Take ownership. Divide and conquer. . . .

Know more about it than it knows about you. They're not as smart as some people think, you know. So they can add up a bunch of six-digit numbers fast — big deal.

Your computer is dead weight without your intervention. Make the best of it.

Index

D

F

Q

R

S

T

🐟 U

Undelete command, 68-69, 147
Undo command, 68, 221
  Ctrl-Z key combination, 64
Units of Measure dialog box, 53
units of measurement, changing, 52-53
upgrading new version, 20-21
user graphics box, 156-157
user groups, 51
utilities
  MSBACKUP, 50

🐟 V

VER (DOS) command, 73
Vertical scroll bar command, 155
View (Ctrl-F3) key combination, 58
View menu, 57, 109, 116, 141, 147, 152,
  155, 184, 187
view modes, 65
viruses
  flashing plaid on-screen, 47
  screen flashing and bombing sound, 97
voices not recording, 173
VRS file extension, 45

🐟 W

/W start-up switch, 31
watermark, 115
WFS files, 136
white space on pages, 114
WIN.INI file, programs making changes,
  221
Windows, unable to find WordPerfect, 59
witch doctors, 6, 89, 113
  avoiding bad advice, 161
  computer professors, 51
  computer sales people, 51
  computer user groups, 51
  data gone forever, 161
  defining, 25
  deleting unknown files, 161
  directory printouts, 89
  error message copies, 89
  experienced coworkers, 51
  explaining your problem, 113
  file backups, 89
  hardware manuals, 89
  having information ready for, 73

on-line computer forums, 51
printouts from CONFIG.SYS,
  AUTOEXEC.BAT, and MSD, 89
program manuals and master disks, 89
rebooting computer, 161
reformatting hard drive, 161
start-up and system disks, 89
technical support staff, 51
what to have ready when doctor arrives,
  89
when to call, 218
where to locate, 51
WordPerfect phone support staff, 51
Yellow Pages, 51
WordPerfect
  beeping, 52
  file formats, 86
  font types supported, 134
  installation, 13-38
  memory requirements, 15, 26
  merging WordPerfect 5.1 files, 211
  no room to install, 15
  quitting without saving, 220
  setup, 39-59
  start-up, 13-38
  unable to find in Windows, 59
  upgrading or installing new version, 20
  version number and release date, 73
  will not start, 21, 22, 23
WordPerfect Shell (Alt-F1) key combination, 65
words, highlighting, 42
words of wisdom, 6
  AUTOEXEC.BAT file, 22
  bar codes, 205
  bookmarks, 76
  button bars, 55
  CHKDSK (DOS) command, 19
  cleaning extraneous data off hard disk,
    19
  CONFIG.SYS file, 22
  DEFRAG (DOS) command, 19
  desktop publishing, 118
  document note types, 110
  environment settings, 55
  fax modems working with WordPerfect,
    191
  font terms, 135
  fonts and document sharing, 140
  function key commands, 65
  Image Editor, 162
  Insert mode, 65

Y

IDG BOOKS WORLDWIDE REGISTRATION CARD

RETURN THIS REGISTRATION CARD FOR FREE CATALOG

Title of this book: S.O.S. For WordPerfect

My overall rating of this book: ❑ Very good [1] ❑ Good [2] ❑ Satisfactory [3] ❑ Fair [4] ❑ Poor [5]

How I first heard about this book:

❑ Found in bookstore; name: [6]   ❑ Book review: [7]

❑ Advertisement: [8]   ❑ Catalog: [9]

❑ Word of mouth; heard about book from friend, co-worker, etc.: [10]   ❑ Other: [11]

What I liked most about this book:

What I would change, add, delete, etc., in future editions of this book:

Other comments:

Number of computer books I purchase in a year: ❑ 1 [12] ❑ 2-5 [13] ❑ 6-10 [14] ❑ More than 10 [15]

I would characterize my computer skills as: ❑ Beginner [16] ❑ Intermediate [17] ❑ Advanced [18] ❑ Professional [19]

I use ❑ DOS [20] ❑ Windows [21] ❑ OS/2 [22] ❑ Unix [23] ❑ Macintosh [24] ❑ Other: [25] _____

(please specify)

I would be interested in new books on the following subjects:
(please check all that apply, and use the spaces provided to identify specific software)

❑ Word processing: [26]   ❑ Spreadsheets: [27]

❑ Data bases: [28]   ❑ Desktop publishing: [29]

❑ File Utilities: [30]   ❑ Money management: [31]

❑ Networking: [32]   ❑ Programming languages: [33]

❑ Other: [34]

I use a PC at (please check all that apply): ❑ home [35] ❑ work [36] ❑ school [37] ❑ other: [38]

The disks I prefer to use are ❑ 5.25 [39] ❑ 3.5 [40] ❑ other: [41]

I have a CD ROM: ❑ yes [42] ❑ no [43]

I plan to buy or upgrade computer hardware this year: ❑ yes [44] ❑ no [45]

I plan to buy or upgrade computer software this year: ❑ yes [46] ❑ no [47]

Name: _____ Business title: [48]

Type of Business: [49]

Address (❑ home [50] ❑ work [51]/Company name: _____)

Street/Suite#

City [52]/State [53]/Zipcode [54]: _____ Country [55]

❑ **I liked this book!**
You may quote me by name in future IDG Books Worldwide promotional materials.

My daytime phone number is _____

IDG BOOKS

THE WORLD OF COMPUTER KNOWLEDGE

❑ YES!

Please keep me informed about IDG's World of Computer Knowledge. Send me the latest IDG Books catalog.